HEALING THE IDENTITY FRACTURE

MANAGING STRATEGIC EXITS AND CAREER REINVENTION

YALE STERN

TABLE OF CONTENTS

LIST OF FIGURES 7
INTRODUCTION 11
   PART I - FROM FRACTURE TO SURVIVAL
      CHAPTER ONE 19
      CHAPTER TWO 25
      CHAPTER THREE 37
      CHAPTER FOUR 49
   PART II - THE CROSSING
      CHAPTER FIVE 63
      CHAPTER SIX 77
   PART III - THE AUTONOMOUS CAREER
      CHAPTER SEVEN 87
      CHAPTER EIGHT 95
      CHAPTER NINE 101
      CHAPTER TEN 117
CONCLUSION 121
   GLOSSARY OF STRATEGIC TERMS 125
   RECOMMENDED READING 129
   SELECTED BIBLIOGRAPHY 133
   METHODOLOGY 137
   ABOUT THE AUTHOR 139
   APPENDIX A: THE ARCHITECT'S WORKBOOK 141
   APPENDIX B: THE CAREER JUDGEMENT CHECKLIST 147

LIST OF FIGURES

Figure 2.1: The Role Exit Trajectory
Conceptual model illustrating the psychological stages of professional role exit, from initial doubt through identity disengagement and separation. *Adapted from* Helen Rose Fuchs Ebaugh, *Becoming an Ex: The Process of Role Exit* (Chicago: University of Chicago Press, 1988).

Figure 2.3: The Five-Stage Career Decay Pattern
Original framework depicting the progressive erosion of professional leverage prior to overt career collapse.

Figure 3.1: The J-Curve of Reinvention
Original model illustrating the temporary decline in status or income that often precedes long-term professional recovery and growth.

Figure 3.2: The Three Simultaneous Collapses
Original synthesis showing the concurrent psychological, economic, and identity disruptions experienced during career fracture.

Figure 4.1: The Limbic System
Simplified schematic illustrating the brain regions involved in perceived social and status threat. *Based on* established neuroscience research (McEwen 2007; Sapolsky 2005).

Figure 4.2: The Hypothalamic-Pituitary-Adrenal (HPA) Axis
Simplified diagram of the hypothalamic–pituitary–adrenal axis and its role in chronic stress and cognitive impairment. *Based on* Bruce S. McEwen, "Physiology and Neurobiology of Stress and Adaptation," *Physiological Reviews* 87, no. 3 (2007).

Figure 5.1: Desperation vs. Strategic Entry
Original comparison illustrating the long-term consequences of panic-driven versus deliberate career entry decisions.

Figure 6.1: The Pareto Efficiency of Learning
Original illustration showing the nonlinear gains produced by focused domain acquisition.

Figure 6.2: The Probability Advantage
Original model demonstrating how combined competencies increase asymmetrical advantage.

Figure 6.3: The Three-Layer Stack Architecture
Original conceptual model extending the Talent Stack Effect by showing how foundational capabilities, applied skills, and strategic leverage form a layered architecture in which professional value compounds - and is constrained - across levels.

Figure 6.4: The Author's Talent Stack
Original visualization of how layered skills create compounded professional value.

Figure 7.1: Linear vs. Exponential Value
Original conceptual comparison between time-bound compensation and scalable value generation.

Figure 7.2: The Hidden Factory Iceberg
Conceptual illustration distinguishing visible outputs from sub-

merged experiential and tacit knowledge. *Informed by* tacit knowledge theory (Michael Polanyi).

Figure 8.1: The Corporate Lifecycle
Original framework illustrating proactive versus reactive career decision paths.

Figure 8.2: The Pre-emptive Strike Payoff Matrix
Original framework illustrating proactive versus reactive career decision paths.

Figure 9.1: The Antifragile Career Curve
Career trajectory model showing how controlled stress and volatility can increase long-term resilience. *Inspired by* Nassim Nicholas Taleb, *Antifragile* (New York: Random House, 2012).

Figure 9.2: Autonomous Income Architecture
Original visualization of diversified income streams designed to reduce dependency on a single employer or role.

Figure 10.1: The Lindy Effect Timeline
Conceptual timeline illustrating increasing durability of practices that persist over time. *Based on* the Lindy Effect as described by Nassim Nicholas Taleb.

Figure 10.2: The Consultant's Curve
Original depiction of diminishing returns from experience-only expertise absent leverage or differentiation.

Table 1: The Autonomous Professional Mindset
Original comparative table contrasting dependent and autonomous career orientations.

INTRODUCTION

THE ARCHITECTURE OF THE AUTONOMOUS PROFESSIONAL

The Death of the Linear Career and the Birth of Antifragility

The traditional career contract is dead.

For a brief, golden period in the mid-20th century, the "Linear Career" was the dominant economic model. The implicit agreement between capital and labor was simple: an individual would acquire a specific set of skills in their early twenties, join a firm, climb a single ladder for forty years, and retire with a pension and a gold watch. Stability was the currency of the day.

That model was a historical anomaly. It was the product of a post-war manufacturing boom and a labor market that valued retention over agility. Today, that model is not only outdated, but also dangerous.

We now live in an economy of disruption. The average lifespan of a company on the S&P 500 has shrunk from 60 years in the 1950s to under 20 years today. Industries rise and fall in the span of a single decade. Skills that are essential today-coding in a specific language, managing a specific supply chain, operating a specific machine-will be automated or outsourced tomorrow.

If you are looking for a straight line, you are looking for a ghost.

The Post-Career Economy

We have entered the **Post-Career Economy**. In this new environment, institutions no longer guarantee continuity, and industries no longer protect expertise. Stability is no longer provided by institutions, and risk has been quietly transferred to individuals.

Yet, despite this volatility, most professionals are still operating with a linear mindset. We define ourselves by a single job title. We anchor our identity to a single industry. When that industry shakes, we crumble. We have not been taught how to pivot; we have only been taught how to climb.

The danger we face today is not unemployment. Unemployment is a temporary economic state. The real danger is **Identity Fracture**, a traumatic psychological break that occurs when your internal definition of "self" is anchored to an external structure that no longer exists. When the job disappears, the identity collapses.

A Note on the Method

I wrote this book to offer an alternative model: **The Lifecycle of Reinvention**. Over the course of forty years, I successfully navigated seven distinct careers across three disparate industries: the performing arts, healthcare, and enterprise technology. I went from the stage to the nursing home, from the social worker's desk to the server room, and from the corporate boardroom to the virtual classroom.

I did not survive this volatility by being the smartest person in the room, nor by having the best connections. I survived by treating my career not as a static identity, but as a dynamic asset portfolio.

This book is not a memoir of luck. It's a manual for survival. It teaches you how to become structurally unbreakable-not emotionally resilient, but economically autonomous.

The Roadmap

This book is structured to guide you through the complete arc of professional reinvention:

Volume I: The Survival

We begin with the immediate reality of the "Zero Point". You will learn how to navigate the "Silent Years" and how to maintain **Internal Dignity** when your external status has evaporated.

Volume II: The Fracture

Once we have stabilized the patient, we perform the **Career Autopsy**. You will learn to identify the five stages of professional decay-from Credential Inflation to Economic Disconnection-that rot a career from the inside out. We will explore the neuroscience of status loss and how to manage the fallout with your family.

Volume III: The Crossing

Here, we get tactical. This is your field manual for the **Humble Entry**. We will explore the J-Curve of Reinvention, providing specific scripts and resume strategies to de-risk your entry into a new industry without losing your soul.

Volume IV: The Autonomous Career

Finally, we move from survival to dominance. We will dismantle the myth that you must be "passionate" to be successful. We will use the **Three-Layer Stack Architecture** to combine disparate skills into a unique "Talent Stack" that makes you mathematically rare. We will construct an **Autonomous Income Architecture** that insulates you from market shocks. And ultimately, we will guide you to the **Soft Landing**-trading your labor for leverage in your final decade.

You are not your job; you are the CEO of a company of one. Welcome to the architecture of your own freedom.

THE CAREER COHERENCE WORKSHEET: A QUICK-START GUIDE

Use this worksheet to establish your baseline before diving into the Seven Transitions.

Current Trajectory Assessment

Identify if your current work is **Compounding** (building durable value) or **Resetting** (trading hours for output).

The Judgment Test: Does my work require me to solve increasingly ambiguous problems, or am I just getting faster at routine tasks?

The Portability Test: If my organization or industry disappeared tomorrow, what specific judgment or context could I carry with me?

The Optionality Test: Does this role increase my future ability to choose, or am I staying because starting over feels too expensive?

Identity & Worth Audit

Distinguish between your professional status and your durable worth.

Status Signal: List your current titles, industry standing, or visible achievements.

Durable Worth: List the judgment, reliability, and ethical restraint you have accumulated that exists *outside* of those titles.

The Fracture Check: Is there a gap between who I am being perceived as and how I actually want to contribute?

Transition Readiness

Determine where you are in the cycle of change.

Survival: Am I currently focused on staying intact and maintaining dignity during a reset?

Stagnation: Am I mistaking professional comfort and familiarity for actual growth?

Restraint: Am I at a stage where I need to start saying "no" to opportunities to protect my energy and focus?

PART I - FROM FRACTURE TO SURVIVAL

CHAPTER ONE

HEALING THE IDENTITY FRACTURE

The Psychology of Career Loss and the Architecture of Reinvention

The Concept: The Sunk Cost Fallacy of the Self

In behavioral economics, the Sunk Cost Fallacy is the tendency to continue investing in a losing project simply because one has already invested heavily in it. The logic is flawed but seductive: "I have spent millions on this factory, so I must keep it open," even if the factory loses money every day.

In our careers, we do the same thing. We simply use a different word for it: "Passion."

We confuse the time we have invested in a career with the future viability of that career. When the market turns against us, we double down rather than pivot. We work harder for less money. We drain our savings to keep the dream alive. We drift into financial and emotional insolvency.

This paralysis is caused by Loss Aversion. Psychologically, the pain of losing our identity is twice as powerful as the pleasure of gaining a new one. We would rather stay in a failing career that feels "like us" than risk a new career that feels like a stranger.

The Diagnosis: What is Identity Fracture?

While "Identity Fracture" is the strategic term we use in this book, the clinical community often refers to this phenomenon as Work-Related Identity Loss. According to research by Conroy & O'Leary-Kelly (2014), losing a career is not just an economic event; it's a "traumatic loss of self-definition." When a professional highly identifies with their role-a state psychologists call Enmeshment-the boundaries between "who I am" and "what I do" dissolve.

Diagnostic Criteria for Identity Fracture

If you are wondering if you are suffering from this condition, examine the following symptoms common in high-functioning professionals facing career decline:

Role-Residual Rumination: An inability to stop thinking about the lost role or industry, even years after leaving.

Status Anxiety: A paralyzing fear of introducing oneself to new people because you can't answer the question, "So, what do you do?"

Values Confusion: A sudden inability to determine what is important to you, because your previous values were dictated by your industry's scorecard.

The "Phantom Limb" Sensation: The instinctive urge to perform tasks associated with your old job, followed by the crashing realization that you no longer have the authority or outlet to do so.

Why You Can't Think Your Way Out of a Career Crisis

We often assume that "Identity Fracture" is a clean break, - like a bone snapping. But in practice, it usually begins as a hairline fissure: the **Identity Crack**.

The Identity Crack is the widening gap between **Who You Are** (your internal narrative) and **Who The Market Says You Are** (your external reality).

Internal Narrative: "I am a respected Director of Operations."

External Reality: "I am currently unemployed and sitting on my couch at 11:00 AM."

The brain abhors this discrepancy. To bridge the gap, the brain initiates a desperate defense mechanism: **Hyper-Rationalization**. You begin to think. You analyze. You replay old meetings. You draft imaginary emails. You spend twelve hours a day "strategizing" your next move.

You tell yourself this is "work." It's not work. It's **Cognitive Spackle**.

You are trying to fill the Identity Crack with thought because you are terrified of the reality on the other side. This is why you feel exhausted despite achieving nothing. You are using 100% of your metabolic energy to mentally sustain a version of yourself that no longer exists physically.

The "Enough Thinking" Threshold There comes a specific moment in every successful reinvention - a moment I call the **"Enough Thinking" Threshold.**

This is the second the professional realizes that *more data will not solve the problem.*

- More introspection will not fix the crack.
- More resume tweaking will not fix the crack.
- More "figuring out my passion" will not fix the crack.

The crack is only sealed by **New Evidence**. And evidence can only be generated by **Action**.

Psychologist Herminia Ibarra calls this "Act-Then-Think." You can't think your way into a new way of acting; you must act your way into a new way of thinking. The Identity Crack closes the moment you stop "strategizing" about being a consultant and actually *sell* one hour of consulting. It closes the moment you stop "worrying" about the new industry and *scrub into* the humble entry role.

Action creates the new identity. Thinking merely mourns the old one.

The Protocol: Seal the Crack If you are currently stuck in the "Silent Years," staring at the ceiling and *thinking* about who you used to be, you are keeping the crack open.

1. **Stop the Autopsy:** You have analyzed the death of your old career enough. Close the file.
2. **Kill the Spackle:** Stop trying to "figure it out." You can't figure out a future you haven't visited yet.

3. **Cross the Threshold:** Do one tangible, low-status thing today that generates real-world data.

The only cure for the fracture is movement.

CHAPTER TWO

THE PSYCHOLOGY OF CAREER DECAY

The Academic Framework: Role Exit Theory

To understand how to move forward, we must look to the work of sociologist Helen Rose Fuchs Ebaugh. In her seminal work on Role Exit Theory, Ebaugh identifies that leaving a major role follows a predictable four-stage trajectory.

1. **First Doubts:** The individual begins to question their commitment to the role. In a career context, this is the "Sunday Night Dread."

2. **Seeking Alternatives:** The individual begins to scan the horizon. This is the brain attempting to build a bridge before the main road collapses.

3. **The Turning Point:** An event occurs that makes staying impossible. This is the Fracture Moment. The old self is dead, but

the new self has not been born.

4. **Creating the Ex-Role:** This is the phase of reconstruction. The individual accepts the label of "Ex-Musician" or "Former Executive" and integrates that past into a new future.

Role Exit Theory

| FIRST DOUBTS | SEEKING ALTERNATIVES | TURNING POINT | CREATING EX-ROLE |

Figure 2.1 *The Role Exit Trajectory Adapted from* Helen Rose Fuchs Ebaugh, *Becoming an Ex* (1988).

Strategic Analysis: Loss vs. Restoration Orientation. How does one move from Stage 3 (Fracture) to Stage 4 (Reconstruction)? Psychologists Stroebe and Schut propose a Dual Process Model of coping. To heal the fracture, you must oscillate between two mindsets:

> **Loss Orientation:** This is the grief work. It's acknowledging the pain, the loss of status, and the sadness of the ending.
>
> **Restoration Orientation:** This is the rebuilding work. It's attending to life changes, doing new things, and distracting oneself from grief.

The Career Autopsy

How Modern Careers Actually Die
(and Why No One Sees It Coming)

The most dangerous myth in the modern marketplace is the belief that career failure is an event. We are conditioned to look for the explosion- the firing, the bankruptcy, the scandalous exit. But careers don't die by explosion. They die by erosion. In the Post-Career Economy, the decay is silent. It's a slow-motion rotting of your economic leverage that occurs while you are still employed, still promoted, and still comfortable. By the time the actual job loss occurs, the career-the mechanism of your long-term value-has been dead for years.

To survive, you must learn to act as a coroner for the living. You must identify the five stages of professional decay while there is still tissue to save.

Phase I: Credential Inflation (The Silent Devaluation)

The first sign of rot is not a loss of money, but a loss of scarcity. You hold a degree or a certification that was once a golden ticket. Ten years ago, it made you special. Today, It's merely the entry fee. The market has minted thousands of replacements who are younger, cheaper, and technically sharper than you.

> **The Symptom:** You notice that entry-level hires have the same qualifications you attained after five years of experience.

> **The Reality:** Your "moat" has been filled in. You are no longer competing on expertise; you are competing on price.

Phase II: Workflow Degradation (The Job Stops Being the Job)

Slowly, the actual creation of value, the work you were hired to do, is displaced by the maintenance of systems. You spend less time designing and more time reporting. You spend less time selling and more time updating the CRM.

> **The Symptom:** Your calendar is full, but your output is empty. You are exhausted by 5:00 PM, yet you can't point to a single asset you created that day.

> **The Reality:** You have been demoted from an "Asset Builder" to a "System Maintainer." You are now a cost center.

Phase III: Compression (When Pay and Power Collapse Inward)

Economic and labor market research suggests that middle coordination roles are being compressed out of modern organizations. This is the stage where the math turns against you. The organization demands more output for the same capital. Raises stop beating inflation. Titles are "flattened" to remove middle management. You are given the responsibilities of a Director with the pay band of a Manager.

The Five-Stage Career Decay Pattern

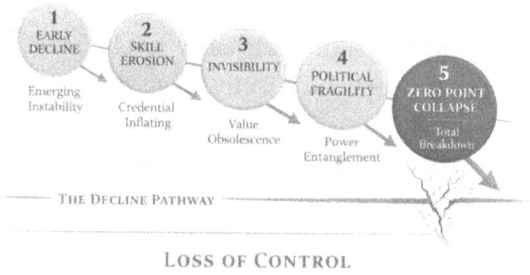

Figure 2.2 The Five-Stage Career Decay Pattern

While digital marketing is beginning to enter a "compression" phase, all the warning signs of a declining industry exist in this space as well. What was once a strategic discipline, requiring a great deal of high-level thinking, has rapidly been reduced to platform operation and dashboard management. The current research on automation suggests that as AI absorbs the execution, people are relegated to either supervising, or worse, becoming obsolete in their ability to create a lasting competitive advantage through the campaign they create. The future of the field will not reward those who "run campaigns", nor will it reward individuals with expertise in using specific tools; these tasks will be completely abstracted behind an interface owned by Google, Meta, Amazon, etc., as each subsequent platform emerges. The research on platform economics indicates that the value created from the use of the platform flows up to the platform owner(s) and down to the lowest cost providers. Therefore, the middle - the career marketer, whose identity is defined by his/her expertise within a specific marketing channel, or by the ability to execute on specific tactics - will slowly disappear. In this environment, the problem is not losing your job; It's developing significant skills in performing a task that the marketplace is no longer willing to pay a premium for, while believing that you are developing significant leverage by constantly doing activities, tracking metrics, and continuously optimizing.

> **The Symptom:** You are asked to "do more with less" for the third year in a row.
>
> **The Reality:** You are being squeezed for margin. Your leverage is gone.

Phase IV: Status Detachment (The Identity Fracture Begins)

This is the psychological break. Your title, which once commanded respect at dinner parties or conferences, begins to feel hollow. The industry buzz has moved to new roles (e.g., "AI Prompt Engineer") while your title (e.g., "SEO Specialist") feels like a relic.

The Symptom: You hesitate when someone asks, "What do you do?" because the answer feels small.

The Reality: Your social capital is depreciating faster than your financial capital.

Phase V: Economic Disconnection (The Fall That Was Already Over)

Finally, the paperwork catches up to the reality. The layoff comes. To you, it's a shock. To the market, it's a correction. The asset was written down years ago; the company is just now closing the ledger.

The Autopsy Files

Real Collapse Reconstructions from the Post-Career Economy

AUTOPSY FILE #1 : Corporate Project Manager

Cause: Credential Inflation + Workflow Degradation + Compression

Analysis: Her job was converted into software while her title remained. She did not lose employment. She lost monopoly.

Many companies today are finding themselves with a redundant structural role of the Corporate Project Manager, not due to fewer projects but rather due to automation of coordination and/or removal of coordination altogether. Planning tools that utilize artificial intelligence (AI) can create project timelines, monitor interdependencies, signal potential risk areas and alert for project deviations before a human intermediary can react, while collaboration platforms have flattened the number of layers of communications that were once necessary for a corporate coordinator to be involved. At the same time, executive teams are looking to reduce overhead costs and discovering a basic fact: the major barrier to decisions is the length of time it takes to make them not their ability to execute on those decisions. As a result, there has been a recent trend of "streamlining" where authority has been passed down to functional leaders, projects have become part of either product or operational responsibilities and the corporate Project Manager's role has shifted from a position of authority to an administrative assistant, always busy, always present but no longer necessary. These types of positions rarely cease to exist during organizational restructuring -- they typically disappear quietly through merger, re-assignment of title or integration into the system(s). This leaves behind very capable individuals who were successful in managing complex processes that no longer occur within a human-based structure.

AUTOPSY FILE #2 : University Lecturer

Cause: Credential Inflation + Status Detachment

Analysis: His value was replaced by adjunct economics. His profession died of margin math.

The automation of higher education will be much like what happened to all other knowledge industries once the content could be separated from the credentialing process. Automated tutoring, adaptive courseware, and self-directed learning platforms can currently provide instructional content, assessments, and automated feedback in ways that no single professor can replicate in terms of both scalability and consistency. Recorded lectures and modular curricula have long since taken the art of teaching and broken it down into reusable products that can be applied to virtually any classroom. With the downward trend of student enrollment, increasing cost of institutions, and public scrutiny of how students are paying for tuition, there are clear incentives for institutions to deconstruct the role of faculty, by keeping a core group of research-active and grant-generating professors, and sending the remaining tasks (teaching) to adjuncts, platforms, or software. Under these conditions, the traditional lecturer, who has traditionally been valued based on their ability to teach a class and not on research, institutional power, or control of the curriculum, will see their role diminished over time. The job will not vanish immediately; however, it will diminish as the result of increased class size, standardized curriculum, asynchronous methods of instruction, and "innovation" projects that silently replace human judgment with system processes. What will remain is not education as mentorship, but education as an infrastructure.

AUTOPSY FILE #3 : Insurance Supervisor

Cause: Workflow Degradation + Compression

Analysis: She was replaced by math.

The insurance business is undergoing transformation based on the use of data, automation, and centralized risk logic. These transformations continue to reduce the supervisory layer that used to translate policy into practice. Insurers now utilize machine learning to perform the functions of underwriting, fraud detection, price adjustment, and claims triage. Machine learning provides a speed and level of consistency in performing these functions that leaves very little opportunity for human decision making. While regulatory reporting, compliance reviews, and performance reviews have historically been the basis for justification for supervisory positions, these responsibilities are now being built into systems as opposed to being managed by individuals. As insurers continue to seek cost reductions and margin protections, the decision-making authority continues to migrate up to Actuaries and Analytics groups, while front line claims handling has become simplified, script-based, or outsourced. Between the automated decision-making of the upper layers of an insurer and the procedural execution of the lower layers, the role of an Insurance Supervisor has evolved into a management-based role, one that is responsible for outcomes over which they do not have control, and managing workflows that will increasingly be self-executing. During restructuring cycles, these positions are rarely completely removed but are instead absorbed, flattened, or re-defined until the supervisory position exists primarily as a title and does not possess either the ability to influence the operation of the insurer or decision-making authority.

AUTOPSY FILE #4 : Digital Marketing Director

Cause: Platformization + Compression

Analysis: Her strategy became dashboards.

AUTOPSY FILE #5 : Hospital Department Manager

Cause: Workflow Degradation + Status Detachment

Analysis: Authority migrated upward into systems.

Conclusion - Research in role-exit theory suggests that careers rarely end suddenly; they decay long before the exit becomes visible. They lose market scarcity. They lose relevance, then leverage, then status, then income. The job ending is only the paperwork. The career was already gone.

The first part of the autopsy process is where many individuals experience a dramatic and disturbing realization: they are no longer participating in a profession in any economically viable manner; however, they are still in the profession mentally. The emotional disconnect from being in a profession (externally) and having a profession (internally), while the other parts of their life (i.e., the work, their title) continue, creates an overwhelming sense of disconnection. Even though their job and title remain, the ability to feel that their efforts align with their identity, which results in a sense of alignment with the rewards of the profession, have gone unnoticed. When these individuals come to realize that the structure of their profession is no longer viable, it's not uncommon for them to become panicked.

These feelings of panic are real, and are physically experienced by each person. For example, a tightness develops in their chest while attending routine meetings. Anxiety increases when reviewing job listings that do not appear to align with their background or skills. Irritability increases, as does their fear of losing time and not having a clear vision for their future. The individual believes they are investing time and energy into a profession that will provide little to nothing of lasting value. However, they do not recognize an alternative, and thus perceive a threat to their well-being, which requires immediate action - typically, the wrong type of action.

The ways in which professionals react during this period are typical and counterproductive. Many professionals choose to invest even more time and energy into a shrinking field in hopes that the more time they put into it, the less likely it will disappear. Other professionals seek out additional education and training through various means such as certifications, "up-skilling" programs, etc. in an attempt to prove that the degree of effort they are putting into their profession will ultimately yield a positive outcome. Some professionals become mired in nostalgia, constantly reliving past successes in hopes that the system will right itself. Other professionals become consumed with comparing themselves to others, i.e. reviewing social media sites (e.g. LinkedIn), and comparing themselves to peers. These comparisons create a false benchmark for success and increase the individual's perception of failure. The worst-case scenario for this period is that it will cause complete paralysis on the individual's part, including an inability to make decisions, constant analysis of the situation, constant planning, and no actual movement toward a solution.

What makes this particular period so particularly hazardous is that the panic seems to be a result of the individual's own failures. As a result, the individual assumes that the panic is a sign of their own inadequacies, rather than a logical reaction to the collapse of a viable market structure. Thus, the individual internalizes what is truly a market signal, and as a result, experiences shame, secrecy, and withdrawal - at the exact same time when they would benefit from clarity and outside input. If left unchecked, the psychological downward spiral caused by the panic can transform what could be a manageable transition to another career into an extended identity crisis.

However, this phase of the process is not pathological. It's a normal reaction to the collapse of a previously held professional paradigm. The discomfort the individual is experiencing is not indicative of a problem with the individual; it's indicative that their internal mental representation of the world is undergoing revision. Panic occurs because the old map of the individual's understanding of the world no longer corresponds to the current environment, and a new map of their understanding of the world has not yet been developed. Essentially, the mind is responding to uncertainty - not failure.

Perhaps most importantly, this phase of the process is not the end of the process; it's the turning point. Once the deterioration of the previous paradigm has been acknowledged and the individual recognizes that there was never a stable base to build upon, then movement toward the future once again becomes a possibility. However, the initial step cannot be at the tactical or ambitious levels. The initial step must be at the level of stabilization: the restoration of dignity, the management of anxiety, and the creation of space to take action without desperation. That work - how to successfully navigate this transitional phase, without further exacerbating the negative consequences - is the focus of the next chapter.

CHAPTER THREE

SURVIVAL AND THE MAINTENANCE OF DIGNITY

Humble Entry And Internal Dignity

The Concept: The Status Trap

When we leave a career, the hardest thing to leave behind isn't the paycheck; it's the Social Capital. We are addicted to "External Dignity"-the respect conferred upon us by our title. The Musician has fans. The Professor has students. When you enter a new industry at the bottom (The Zero Point), that external feedback loop is severed. You become invisible.

This creates a Status Trap. Many professionals refuse to pivot because they can't bear the optical drop in status. They would rather be an unemployed "Director" than an employed "Assistant." This vanity is the enemy of reinvention.

The Psychology: Internal vs. External Dignity

To survive The Zero Point, you must engineer a shift to Internal Dignity. In his memoir Man's Search for Meaning, Viktor Frankl argues that dignity is not a circumstance; it's a choice. It's the "last of the human freedoms"-to choose one's attitude in any given set of circumstances.

- **External Dignity:** "I am valuable because I am leading this meeting." (Fragile).

- **Internal Dignity:** "I am valuable because I am performing this task-no matter how small-with excellence and humanity." (Antifragile).

The Olfactory Wall: A First-Person Account of the Zero Point

We talk about "status loss" in economic terms. We track it on spreadsheets and LinkedIn profiles. But status loss is not an intellectual event. It's a sensory one.

For me, the Identity Fracture didn't happen when the music gigs dried up. It didn't happen when I looked at my bank account. It happened the moment the automatic doors slid open at the nursing home.

It was the smell.

You think you know what a nursing home smells like. You have heard the jokes about boiled cabbage and rubbing alcohol. But unless you have worked the floor, you have no idea. The smell is profound. It's a physical weight. It's a thick, chemical cocktail of industrial Pine-Sol, over-cooked food, and the undeniable, sweet-sick scent of human decay. It's the smell of biology winning the war against dignity.

I wasn't entirely naive. I had cared for my mother as she died of cancer. I had been introduced to the mechanics of the end-the fluids, the pain, the slow shrinking of a world into a single room. I thought that experience had prepared me. I thought I had "paid my dues" to mortality.

I was wrong. Caring for a loved one is a tragedy; working in a facility is an industry.

The Erasure of the Self

I walked to the nurses' station to report for my first shift. I was wearing generic scrubs. I had no badge yet.

"I'm the new orderly," I said.

The nurse didn't look up. She pointed to a cart of linens and a list of room numbers. "Start with 204. Bed change. Then he needs a transfer to the chair."

In that moment, twelve years of my life evaporated.

Nobody here knew I was a musician. Nobody knew I had stood on stages and controlled the energy of a room. Nobody knew I had fans, or recordings, or a "name." To the woman behind the desk, I was not a person with a history. I was a set of hands. I was a functional asset, and a low-value one at that.

This is the terror of The Zero Point. When we are high on the career ladder, we mistake our context for our character. We think people respect *us*. They don't. They respect our context-our title, our budget, our proximity to power. When you strip the context away, you find out exactly how much "social gravity" you actually generate. In the nursing home, my gravity was zero.

The Descent

- My shift was a tour of things polite society pretends don't exist. I walked into Room 204. The resident was an elderly man, withered by age, curled into a fetal position. He was crying-not the dramatic sobbing of movies, but the low, confused keening of dementia. He didn't know where he was. He didn't know who I was. He had soiled himself.

The task was mechanical. Roll the patient. Remove the sheets. Clean the skin. Replace the sheets. Roll the patient back.

- But the psychology was brutal. My ego-the "Musician"-was screaming. *I am better than this,* it shouted. *I am an artist. I deal with aesthetics, with beauty, with high concepts. I don't wipe bodies.*

The smell was overwhelming. I had to breathe through my mouth to keep from gagging. I felt a flush of hot shame, not just for myself, but for the man in the bed. He was exposed. He was helpless. And I was the anonymous witness to his final humiliation.

The Death of the Musician

Somewhere around the fourth hour of that first shift, "The Musician" finally died. I realized that if I kept holding onto my old identity, I wasn't going to survive this shift, let alone the month. The gap between "Who I think I am" (an Artist) and "Who I am economically" (an Orderly) was too wide. It was tearing me apart. I had to let him go. I had to let the stage go.

This is the essence of Identity Fracture. It's the painful snap that occurs when you realize your past assets are liabilities in your present reality. My ability to play a scale or read a crowd meant nothing here. The only thing that mattered was: *Can I clean this man with gentleness? Can I transfer this woman to her chair without hurting her?*

The Birth of Procedural Dignity

That afternoon, I discovered the only tool that works at the bottom of the ladder. I discovered Procedural Dignity.

I couldn't get dignity from my title. "Orderly" commands no respect.

I couldn't get dignity from the environment. The environment was depressing.

I couldn't get dignity from the "audience." The audience was confused and dying.

I had to manufacture dignity from the process itself. I decided that I would make the bed corners perfectly sharp. Not because anyone checked, but because *I* did it. I decided I would speak to the dementia patients with the same cadence and respect I would use for a venue promoter. Not because they understood me, but because *I* needed to hear it.

I told myself: *"I am not cleaning a mess. I am restoring order to a chaotic universe."*

It sounds trivial. But it saved me. By focusing on the micro-excellence of the task—the smoothness of the sheet, the gentleness of the hand—I built a new identity. I wasn't a "Failed Musician." I was a "Competent Man."

The View from the Bottom

As the weeks turned into months, something strange happened. Because I was invisible, I became all-seeing.

Doctors would stand next to me and discuss patient files as if I were furniture. Nurses would complain about the administrative software while I mopped the floor. Administrators would leave sensitive intake forms on the desk while I emptied the trash.

I began to see the **Hidden Factory**.

I saw that the intake process was broken-nurses were writing data on paper, then walking it to a computer, then typing it in. It was a 20-minute waste of time per patient. I saw that the supply closet inventory was always wrong because the checkout sheet was too complicated. I saw that the doctors didn't actually know which patients were "high risk" for falls; they were guessing based on outdated charts.

I started taking notes. Not as an orderly, but as a spy.

I realized that while the doctors understood medicine, and the nurses understood care, *nobody understood the system*. The system was a mess of disconnected parts, and I was the only one traveling between all of them.

That realization was the seed of my next career. I didn't know it yet, but I wasn't just mopping floors. I was acquiring the Domain Knowledge that would eventually allow me to build the IT systems that ran the entire facility.

But it started with the smell. It started with the death of my ego in Room 204.

If you are currently standing in the wreckage of your own career, looking at a job that feels "beneath" you, smell the air. Take it in. That repulsion you feel is just your old self dying. Let it die. There is work to be done.

The Strategy: Domain Acquisition as "Tuition"

Why take a minimum wage job? To the strategist, this is not "labor"; it's Paid Tuition. Every industry has a Hidden Curriculum-the unwritten rules of how money is made and how power flows. You can't learn this in an MBA program. You can only learn it by being in the trenches.

This is the Humble Entry Strategy.

> **The Transaction:** You trade your time (and your ego) for Domain Acquisition.
>
> **The Advantage:** You are an "Undercover Boss" in your own life. Because you are low-status, people speak freely around you. You see the inefficiencies, the waste, and the "Hidden Factory" that management never sees.

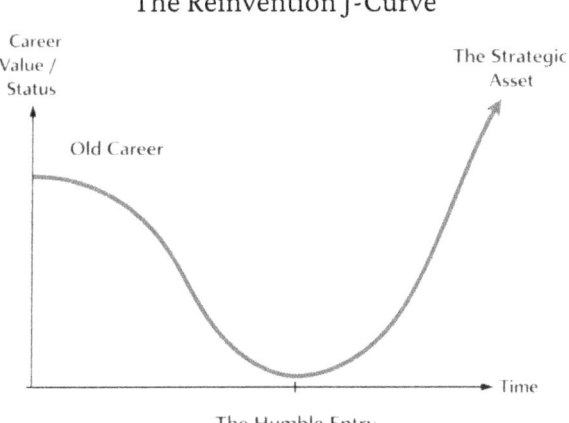

Figure 3.1 *The J-Curve of Reinvention*

The subject didn't just change bedpans; he studied the workflow of the nurses. He watched how the intake forms were processed. He learned the medical terminology. He was performing Ethnographic Research. He was "buying" the data he would later use as a Systems Administrator to automate their jobs.

He couldn't have built the system if he hadn't first swept the floor.

The J-Curve of Reinvention

Economically, a Humble Entry follows a J-Curve:

The Drop (Phase 1): You voluntarily lower your status and income to enter the new field. This feels like a crash.

The Valley (Phase 2): You are at the bottom. This is the "Zero Point." This is where you acquire Domain Knowledge.

The Ascent (Phase 3): You apply your previous "Talent Stack" (e.g., Logic, Management) to your new Domain Knowledge.

The Breakout (Phase 4): You rise past your original peak. You are no longer just an "Orderly"; you are an "Orderly who understands Systems." You bypass the standard career ladder because you have unique data.

The Lesson: You must be willing to look like a loser in the short term to be a winner in the long term.

The Silent Years

The Psychological and Economic No-Man's Land After Career Collapse

Once you've lost your career, you're entering a phase that your college or HR department has likely failed to warn you about. The "Silent Years" are the void between identities, and they can be incredibly frightening. The Silent Years are a period of total erasure of your identity as "the VP of Sales". The Silent Years represent the time when all the external validation loops (that supported your ego for so long) will disappear. Your phone won't ring. Your email box will no longer refresh. And the social gravity that was holding you in place will disappear.

A large number of people who find themselves in this position panic. Many people seek to fill the "void" created by their loss of employment with "noise" - frantic networking, desperate application, "busy work", etc. This is a bad strategy. The Silent Years are NOT a time of transition. .. they are a time of transformation. If you panic during this time, you will disintegrate. If you create a strategy to use the Silent Years effectively, you will transform and emerge.

The Three-Front War

Figure 3.2 *The Three Simultaneous Collapses*

The Three Simultaneous Collapses

You are not only dealing with being unemployed... you are dealing with a three-front attack:

Economic Collapse: The economic collapse represents the obvious wound. However, it is usually the easiest wound to treat using some type of short term savings or survival jobs.

Social Collapse: Your status signaling is now off line. You are finding out painful truths about your "friends" from work - they were not really friends... they were simply proximity based associates. Once the proximity to them is gone... the associate relationship will also be gone.

Psychological Collapse: This is typically the most deadly. You are no longer provided with the "temporal structure" of a 9 to 5 work schedule. You are now forced to deal with fractured perceptions of time - days become indistinguishable from weeks. You are no longer able to tell the world what your story is... you have lost the "narrative coherence" associated with your job title.

The Zero Point Rules

In order to survive this wasteland, you will need to follow a wartime code of conduct:

Rule One: Embrace Invisibility. Accept invisibility. You will feel like you are invisible. Don't fight it. Use it. Invisibility is a cloak that provides you the opportunity to retrain, to fail, and to pivot without an audience. You are not "unemployed"... you are in stealth mode.

Rule Two: Dignity is Procedural. Dignity is procedural. You are going to have to manufacture dignity through procedure since you will no longer be able to get it from your job title. You are going to wake up at 6:00 AM not because you have a boss... but because you are a professional. You are going to dress for the day not because you have a meeting... but because you want to. You will be able to find dignity in the consistency of your daily routine. .. rather than the outcome of your activities.

Rule Three: Survival Precedes Reinvention. Survival precedes reinvention. You should not be trying to "find your passion" while you are hemorrhaging money. First, stabilize the cash flow. A starving strategist makes poor strategic decisions. Get the "survival job", stop the financial bleeding, and then begin to plan your future.

End-of-Chapter Reflection Prompt

Identity: What part of your "internal identity" are you currently asking to go dormant to fit your "institutional identity"?

CHAPTER FOUR

THE PHYSIOLOGY OF LOSS

Why Career Collapse Feels Like Dying
(The Neuroscience of Status)

Well-meaning friends say things like, "It's just a job, you're more than your title. One door closes, another opens." Friends are wrong - both literally and scientifically.

Loss of a job is seen as an economic event by your conscious mind. However, to your limbic system, the emotional core of your brain, losing status is a survival threat. The pain you experience during Identity Fracture is not figurative - it is real and quantifiable.

You cannot develop strategies to overcome a situation until you understand the biological basis of falling.

The Social Pain Overlap

In 2003, Naomi Eisenberger and Matthew Lieberman used functional magnetic resonance imaging (fMRI) to study the social exclusion of subjects. What they expected to be activated in the subjects' emotional processing centers, instead were activated in the Anterior Cingulate Cortex (ACC).

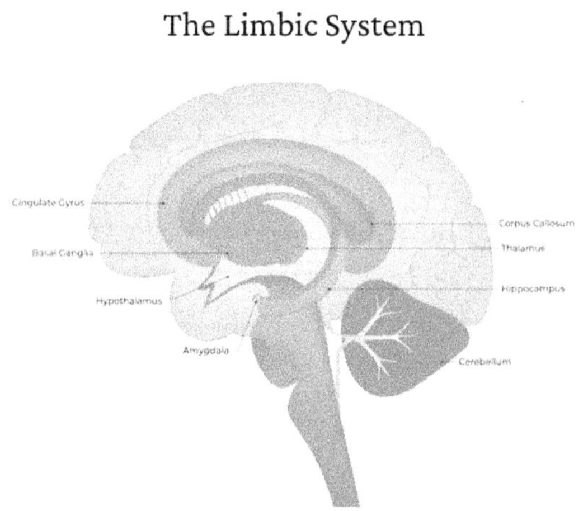

The Limbic System

Figure 4.1 The Limbic System

The ACC is the same part of the brain that registers physical pain - when you break your leg, the ACC is active. When you lose standing within the tribe (your job), the ACC is active. To the human brain, Social Pain = Physical Pain.

From an evolutionary standpoint, it would be logical for humans to perceive status loss as a survival threat. Being ostracized from the tribe in prehistoric times could result in starving to death or being preyed upon by predators. Therefore, the brain developed to register status loss as a physical threat. It releases the same distress signals as a crushed leg.

This explains why Identity Fracture feels so debilitating. You feel heavy. Your chest hurts. You are tired. You are not "sad," you are in shock. Your brain is treating the loss of your job as if you had been mauled by a bear.

The Cortisol Fog

While the ACC registers the pain, your endocrine system handles the panic. When your identity is threatened, the Hypothalamus-Pituitary-Adrenal (HPA) axis is triggered. Cortisol, the body's primary stress hormone, floods your system. In short bursts, cortisol is useful; it helps you run from a tiger. However, the threat posed by a career crisis does not disappear in ten minutes. The threat lasts for months. You become chronically hypercortisolemic. This state is lethal to strategy because of what it does to the **Prefrontal Cortex (PFC)**. The PFC is the CEO of

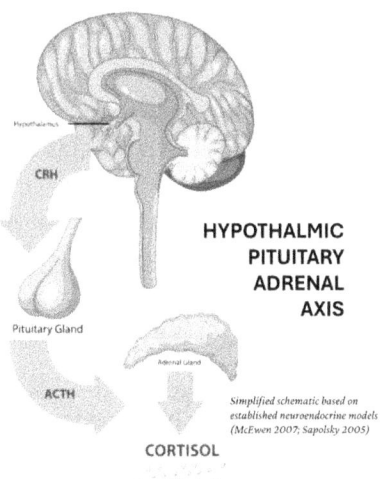

Figure 4.2 The Hypothalamic-Pituitary-Adrenal (HPA) Axis

your brain. It's responsible for logic, long term planning and managing emotions. High levels of cortisol will shut down the Prefrontal Cortex. This is referred to as the "Cortisol Fog." This is why, right after a layoff, you find yourself staring at a blank Word document for three hours, unable to write a simple cover letter. This is why you snap at your partner. This is why you impulsively make poor financial decisions. You are attempting to engage in complex strategic planning (reinventing yourself) with a brain that has been chemically lobotomized to only respond to threats of immediate survival.

The Primate Status Drop

Biologist Robert Sapolsky studied the decline in status among primate males. When a dominant male falls in status, his serotonin levels drop and his cortisol levels increase. As a result of these changes, he becomes weakened immunologically and withdraws.

Like primates in suits, we consider ourselves sophisticated. However, in the business world, we exist in a hierarchy where "vice president" is alpha and "unemployed" is an outcast. When you lose the alpha title, your biology responds as if you had been demoted from alpha. You suffer a significant reduction in Serotonin (confidence neurotransmitter) and Dopamine (reward neurotransmitter).

This causes the "phantom limb" sensation of your career. You reach for your phone to check non-existent emails (to receive a dopamine rush). You enter a room feeling less substantial (serotonin crash). You are experiencing withdrawal symptoms from neurochemicals.

The Strategic Implication:
Biology First, Strategy Second

Most individuals attempt to battle their biology with "will power." They force themselves to sit at the computer for eight hours a day searching for jobs, while their ACC screams and their PFC is offline. This results in burnout and suboptimal interviews. People can smell the desperation (cortisol) coming off of you.

An Autonomous Professional understands the biology. Before you can design your new career, you need to stabilize the animal.

The Recovery Protocol:

1. **Acknowledge the Injury:** Do not tell yourself, "it's just a job." During the first month of Identity Fracture, treat it like you would a surgical recovery. You are hurt. Be prepared to produce less.

2. **Flush the Cortisol:** There is no way to "think" cortisol away. You need to metabolize it. High intensity exercise is not optional during a career transition, it is the only way to turn your PFC back on.

3. **Manufacture Serotonin:** Since you are no longer receiving serotonin through external validation ("status"), you must receive it from internal validation ("micro-wins"). This is why the Humble Entry method works. Completing a task, such as cleaning a room, gives you a small serotonin boost. It helps stabilize your neurochemistry.

Do not construct a skyscraper on a foundation that is currently liquefied. Repair the biology. Then, construct the tower.

The Family Meeting

Managing the Social Fallout of a Strategic Pivot

There is a reason many Autonomous Professionals fail before they ever reach the "Zero Point." It's not because they lack the skills. It's not because the market rejected them.

It's because they were sabotaged in their own kitchen.

When you decide to execute a **Humble Entry** (Chapter 3)-voluntarily dropping your title and income to acquire new leverage-you are not the only one who pays the price. Your partner and your children pay it too. To you, the pivot is a strategic maneuver. To your family, it looks indistinguishable from a crisis. If you attempt to navigate the "Silent Years" without the explicit, signed-off consent of your household, you are fighting a two-front war. You are fighting the market by day, and you are fighting a "Proxy War" at home by night. You will lose.

The Hidden Asset: Spousal Status

We like to believe that our partners love us simply for "who we are." This is true, but it's incomplete. In a marriage, your career is a Joint Asset. Your title does not just confer status upon you; it confers status upon your partner. When you are "The Director," your partner is "The Director's Partner." It provides narrative coherence at dinner parties. It provides a sense of future security.

When you come home and say, *"I'm quitting the Director job to become an entry-level Analyst in a new field,"* you are not just depreciating your own asset. You are depreciating *theirs*. You are introducing two toxic elements into the family system:

1. **Economic Anxiety:** "Will we lose the house?"

2. **Social Embarrassment:** "What do I tell my parents? What do I tell our friends?"

If you don't address the second point, the first point will become a weapon. Your partner will argue about "budget" when they are actually panicked about "status."

The Error: Asking for Permission vs. Presenting a Prospectus

Most professionals botch this conversation because they approach it like a child asking a parent for permission.

The Weak Approach: "I'm really unhappy. I think I want to quit and try something else. Is that okay?"

This places the burden of your happiness on your partner. If they say "No," they are the villain. If they say "Yes," they own the risk. It's unfair leadership.

The Autonomous Professional approaches this not as a partner venting, but as a **CEO presenting to the Board**. You don't ask for permission to have feelings; you present a **Prospectus for Reinvestment**.

The Protocol: The "Board Meeting"

Don't have this conversation while doing the dishes. Don't have it in the car. Schedule it. Treat it with the gravity of a merger acquisition.

Step 1: The Diagnosis (The Depreciation Warning)

You must frame the current "safe" job not as a stable asset, but as a declining one.

> ***The Script:*** "I want to review the family balance sheet. Right now, we rely on my income as a [Current Role]. We treat this as safe. However, looking at the market trends (Chapter 2.1), this asset is depreciating. If I stay here five more years, my value will be zero. We are currently 'shorting' our own future."

Step 2: The Proposal (The J-Curve)

Show them the J-Curve diagram (Figure 2.1). Explain that you are not "quitting"; you are reallocating capital.

> ***The Script:*** "To secure our future, I need to move into [New Industry]. To do that, I must take a temporary step back. I am trading short-term income/status for long-term equity. We will take a hit in Year 1 (The Valley), to ensure we are solvent in Year 10 (The Breakout)."

Step 3: The "Stop-Loss" Agreement

This is the most critical step. You must de-risk the pivot for your partner. You can't ask them to sign up for indefinite struggle. You must give them a Kill Switch.

> ***The Script:*** "I am asking for a 12-month runway. Here is the exact budget we will live on. If, by [Date], I have not reached [Income Benchmark] or secured [Specific Role], I agree to trigger the Stop-Loss. I will return to the old industry and take a standard job. We are capping the downside."

Handling the "Dinner Party" Problem

Your partner is likely terrified of the question: "So, what is your husband/wife doing these days?"

You must give them a narrative shield. Don't let them say, "He's trying to find himself."

Give them a script that sounds active and strategic:

> *The Script:* "He's consulting on a project in the [New Industry] space while restructuring his portfolio. He's moving into the 'High-Leverage' phase of his career."

The Contract

When the partner feels heard, protected by a Stop-Loss, and armed with a social script, they shift from "Saboteur" to "Stakeholder." You need them in the foxhole with you. The "Silent Years" are lonely enough. Don't make them lonely in your own home.

Interlude A: The Dictionary of Corporate Euphemisms

A Translation Guide for the Autonomous Professional

In the Post-Career Economy, language is often used not to convey meaning, but to obscure risk. Organizations use a specific dialect-"Corporate speak"-to soften the harsh economic realities of the employment contract. To survive, you must learn to translate the "Official Factory" language into "Hidden Factory" reality.

We are a family

- **Official Definition:** We care about you beyond your economic output.

- **Strategic Translation:** We expect you to work unpaid overtime (emotional labor) and blur the boundaries between your personal life and our profit margins. Note: Families don't fire their children when quarterly revenue misses projections.

Unlimited Paid Time Off (PTO)

- **Official Definition:** You have the freedom to take as much rest as you need.

- **Strategic Translation:** We have removed the accrued liability of vacation pay from our balance sheet. Because there is no "bank" of days, you will psychologically police yourself and likely take fewer days than before to avoid looking "uncommitted."

Performance Improvement Plan (PIP)

- **Official Definition:** A structured plan to help a struggling employee get back on track.

- **Strategic Translation :** A paperwork trail designed to limit legal liability before a pre-determined firing. It's not a rehabilitation tool; it's an eviction notice.

Stretch Assignment

- **Official Definition:** A challenging project designed to help you grow.

- **Strategic Translation:** A temporary promotion without the corresponding pay raise. We are testing to see if you will do two jobs for the price of one.

Right-Sizing / Restructuring

- **Official Definition:** Aligning our workforce with current business needs.

- **Strategic Translation:** We made a bad strategic bet, and you are the liquidity we are using to cover the loss.

Human Resources

- **Official Definition:** The department dedicated to employee well-being.

- **Strategic Translation:** The department dedicated to protecting the company *from* the employees. Don't confuse HR with a therapist or a union.

Golden Handcuffs

- **Official Definition:** Unvested stock options designed to reward longevity.

- **Strategic Translation:** A retention fee paid to prevent you from discovering your true market value on the open market.

Exit Interview

- **Official Definition:** An opportunity for you to give honest feedback to improve the culture.

- ***Strategic Translation:*** A final risk assessment to ensure you are not planning to sue us. Anything you say here can only hurt you.

End-of-Chapter Reflection Prompt

Survival: What unglamorous labor are you currently doing that deserves more self-respect than you are giving it?

PART II - THE CROSSING

CHAPTER FIVE

THE HUMBLE ENTRY FIELD MANUAL

How to Enter a New Industry Without Destroying Your Dignity

The biggest barrier to reinventing yourself is not the lack of skills you have, but the excess of pride you have. You don't want to start at the bottom of the industry because it is seen as a step backward. However, starting at the bottom is not a step back; it is paid reconnaissance.

When you enter a new field at the zero point (at the entry-level), you are not just a worker. You are a spy. You have entered into the hidden factory with a clearance level that no one within the organization has.

The Strategy: Strategic Entry vs. Desperation Entry

> **Desperation Entry:** You take a lower-paying job to support your living expenses. You hate the job. You hide your identity. You wait until you can be rescued. Outcome: Wage captivity long-term.

Strategic Entry: You take a lower-paying job to map out the territory. You complete the task with integrity and gain the trust of others. However, while you are completing the task you are thinking about the systems you are working within. You are looking for the friction points, waste, and tribal knowledge that is not documented. Outcome: Leverage acceleration and rebirth.

Don't choose a role based on comfort or "transferable skills." Choose a role based on Friction and Bottleneck Proximity.

Avoid: Receptionist, Greeters, Isolated Data Entry Clerk. These positions are ornamental and view nothing.

Target: Dispatchers, Intake Coordinators, Expeditors, Help Desk. These positions are friction positions. They are located at the crossroads where the business breaks.

The Mission: Map the Money

From your vantage point at the bottom, you must answer three questions that the CEO can't answer:

1. Where does the data *actually* go? (Not where the chart says it goes).

2. Who *actually* fixes the problems? (The "Shadow IT" network).

3. What is the unspoken rule that keeps this place running?

When you submit your application for the next rung up the corporate ladder, you won't be applying as a candidate. You will be applying as a diagnostician. You will be offering solutions that only someone who has worked at the bottom of the corporation could know. You don't climb the corporate ladder. You circumvent it by becoming the system.

The Stealth Resume - How to De-Risk Your Competence for a Humble Entry

If you are attempting a Humble Entry (going from a high status job, such as director of operations to a low status job, such as logistics coordinator to obtain domain knowledge), there may be something confusing happening to you. You may be being turned down not because you don't qualify for the position, but because you are too qualified.

To the hiring manager, an overqualified candidate is not an asset; they are a **Flight Risk**.

The hiring manager looks at your resume and thinks:

1. "They will get bored in month two."

2. "They will try to take my job in month four."

3. "They will leave for a better offer in month six."

In order to make the Humble Entry, you need to be able to create a stealth resume. A stealth resume is designed to hide your true experience by reframing your past from "strategy" to "utility". You want to appear as a pair of hands, not as a threat.

The Three Laws of De-Escalation

1. The Title Downgrade

HR algorithms and hiring managers are status-matchers. If they are hiring a "Coordinator," and they see "Vice President" on your resume, the cognitive dissonance triggers an automatic rejection.

- The Fix: You must functionally describe your role rather than using the official title.

- *Instead of:* "Senior Vice President of Global Sales"

- *Use:* "Sales Team Lead" or "Account Manager."

- *Ethical Note:* This is not lying if the functional description is accurate. You managed accounts. You led a team. You are simply removing the "inflation" that scares the hiring manager.

2. The Verb Swap (Strategy vs. Execution)

High-level resumes use "Strategic Verbs" (Directed, Architected, Visioned). Low-level resumes use "Tactical Verbs" (Processed, Updated, Scheduled).

- *Bad (Too Strategic):* "Architected a global logistics overhaul saving $2M."

- *Good (Stealth):* "Processed daily logistics manifests and updated tracking spreadsheets for 500+ shipments."

- *Why this works:* It tells the manager, *"I am not here to rewrite your strategy; I am here to clear your inbox."*

3. The Narrative Bridge (The Cover Letter)

You must address the elephant in the room immediately. Why does a former Director want to answer phones? If you don't explain it, they will assume the worst (you were fired, you are desperate, or you are crazy).

- **The Script:** *"After 15 years in high-stress management, I am intentionally seeking a role where I can focus on execution and individual contribution. I miss the satisfaction of tangible work and am looking for stability rather than a ladder."*

- This frames your "demotion" as a **lifestyle choice**, which HR understands and accepts.

The "Functional Format" Trap

Don't use a "Chronological Resume" which highlights your career progression (and thus your high status). Use a "Functional Resume" which highlights specific skills.

- **Section 1: Core Competencies.** (e.g., "Inventory Management," "CRM Data Entry").

- **Section 2: Professional History.** (Keep the dates, but minimize the descriptions).

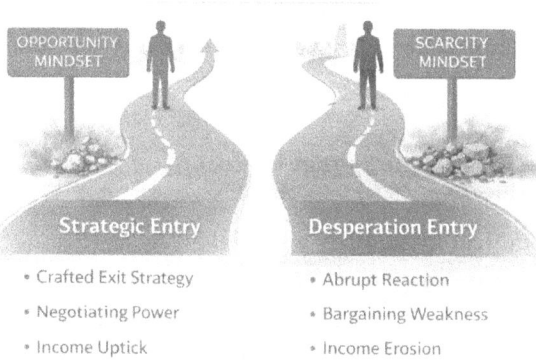

Figure 5.1 Desperation vs. Strategic Entry

This structure forces the reader to look at what you can do, not who you used to be.

THE FIRST 90 DAYS

The Velocity Protocol for the Zero Point

Congratulations! You've made it through Chapter 3.1, the Stealth Resume. You've bitten the bullet, taken the pay-cut and landed a lower-echelon position in your new field. You're now standing at The Zero Point.

This is the most dangerous juncture of the pivot.

If you are too passive you will be stuck in the entry-level role for years. You'll become "the best dishwasher" instead of "the future restaurant owner."

If you are too aggressive, you will elicit the "Corporate Immune System." You will appear to be an arrogant "know-it-all" who believes they're superior to the work.

You must use a Velocity Protocol to survive. Your objective is not to perform the job. Your objective is to hack the job. You're not an employee. You're a sleeper agent.

Phase 1: Weeks 1–4 (The Sponge Protocol)

Objective: Radical Invisibility and Dialect Acquisition.

Your instinct will be to prove your value immediately. You will see a broken process on Day 3 and say, "In my old industry, we did it this way."

Don't do this. If you speak too soon, you reveal yourself as an outsider. You have not earned the political capital to critique the culture.

- **Zero Suggestions:** Don't make a suggestion. Don't tweak a spreadsheet. Don't contribute to a discussion unless directly asked.

- **Acquire the Dialect:** Each industry has its own vocabulary. In tech, it's "agile/sprint". In healthcare, it's "HIPAA/triage." In logistics, it's "last mile." Pay attention. Take notes. Parrot phrases until you sound native.

- **Identify the "Shadow Boss":** Examine the organizational chart. Compare that to reality. Whose input determines decisions? That person is the Shadow Boss. Your objective is to build rapport with the Shadow Boss, not the manager.

The Deliverable: By the end of Week 4, you should be able to do the core job without asking for help, and you should know the names of the Shadow Boss's children.

Phase 2: Weeks 5–8 (The Cartographer Protocol)

Objective: Map the Hidden Factory.

Now that you are trusted as "a safe pair of hands," you can begin the real work: Espionage. You are looking for the Hidden Factory (Chapter 5)-the messy reality of how the business actually runs.

- **Find the "Swivel Chair" Interface:** Identify any function where a person takes data from one screen and types it into another. That is a weakness. That is your opening.

- **Find the "Magic Spreadsheet":** Every department uses a large, secret Excel file that IT does not understand. It holds the truth. Find it. Figure out the macros.

- **Find the "Third Rail":** What was the one misstep that got the previous guy canned? (i.e. "never respond to the client without copying the account executive"). Learn what cannot be done.

The Deliverable: By the end of Week 8, you should have a private document listing the top three inefficiencies in the department, ranked by "Pain Level" vs. "Fix Difficulty."

Phase 3: Weeks 9–12 (The Sniper Protocol)

Objective: The First Strike.

You have been silent for 60 days. You have done the grunt work. You speak the dialect. Now, you strike. You are going to pick one problem from your Cartographer list - specifically, a "High Pain / Low Difficulty" problem - and solve it.

- **Build in Secret:** Don't ask for permission. Build the macro, the checklist, or the script at home or during lunch.

- **The "Columbo" Reveal:** Do not describe it as a "strategic initiative." Describe it as an accidental discovery.

- **The Script:** "Hey [Shadow Boss], I observed everyone working late to fix formatting problems with reports. I was messing around this weekend and wrote a little script that automates that part of the report. I tested it on my own files and it worked. Want me to send it to you?"

- Hand it off. Allow the Shadow Boss to take credit if he wants. You don't care about the credit; you care about the reputation.

The Shift: The moment that script works, your identity shifts. You are no longer "The New Guy". You are "The Guy Who Fixed Reports." You have shifted from Volume II (The Crossing) to Volume III (The Autonomous Career). You have successfully elevated from a laborer to an asset.

The Trap: The "Competence Curse"

A warning: If you're too good at the entry-level work, they'll never promote you. They need you there.

- **The Strategic Balance:** Be "good enough" at the grunt work so as to avoid being fired, but be "exceptional" at the high-leverage work (intrapreneurship).

- Don't be the fastest digger. Be the person who invents the shovel.

The 90-Day Review

When you sit down for your official 3-month review, the conversation should not be about your job description.

- *Old Script:* "I have hit my targets and learned the system."

- *Strategic Script:* "I've hit my targets. I also identified a workflow bottleneck that was costing the team 10 hours a week, and I deployed a fix that reclaimed that time. I'd like to discuss how we can apply that logic to the rest of the department."

You are no longer interviewing for the job you have. You are interviewing for the job you are creating.

INTERLUDE B: TWO TIMELINES

A Day in the Life: The Tenant vs. The Landlord

The difference between a Linear Careerist and an Autonomous Professional is not usually intelligence or talent. It's **Ownership**.

The Linear Careerist acts like a Tenant. They live in a career owned by someone else. They are subject to eviction. They fix the landlord's plumbing for free.

The Autonomous Professional acts like a Landlord. They own the career. The employer is merely the tenant paying rent (salary) for their skills.

Here is how that mindset shift alters the physiology of a single Tuesday: (*See page 68*)

The Analysis:

The Tenant is exhausted because they are sustaining a façade. They are burning energy trying to look busy and safe.

The Landlord is energized because they are building equity. Every hour of work is either generating cash (salary) or leverage (skills/assets).

The Tenant hopes the roof doesn't leak. The Landlord fixes the roof because they own the building.

CHAPTER FIVE | 73

Time	The Tenant (Linear)	The Landlord (Autonomous)
6:30 AM	Wakes up. Immediately checks phone. Cortisol spike due to an urgent email from a boss sent at 11 PM.	Wakes up. Does not touch phone. 30 minutes of exercise to regulate the HPA axis (flush cortisol).
8:00 AM	Commutes (or logs on) in a state of reactive anxiety, mentally rehearsing defenses for a meeting.	Opens a personal laptop. Spends 60 minutes working on "The Leverage Bucket" (a side project, a course, or an article). Pays themselves first.
9:00 AM	Logs into the corporate slack. Says "Good morning!" to signal visibility. Immediately starts clearing the inbox (other people's priorities).	Logs into the corporate slack. Scans for "Signal" vs. "Noise." Ignores non-critical emails. Begins deep work on a "Black Box" project (Volume IV).
11:00 AM	**Meeting:** "Strategy Sync." Sits quietly, afraid to speak up, hoping not to get assigned more work. Takes notes.	**Meeting:** "Strategy Sync." Listens for "Hidden Factory" problems. Identifies a broken process. Offers to fix it using a script they already wrote (The Intrapreneur).
1:00 PM	Lunch at desk while replying to emails. Feels "busy" but accomplished nothing tangible.	Lunch away from screens. Listens to a podcast on a *different* industry to expand Domain Knowledge (Chapter 1).
3:00 PM	Energy crash. Scrolls social media. Feels guilty. Updates a spreadsheet manually because "that's how we do it."	Automates the spreadsheet using a new tool. Uses the saved time to document the process (building a SOP asset).
5:30 PM	Boss asks for a last-minute report. Tenant says "Yes" instantly, fearing for job security. Cancels gym plans.	Boss asks for a last-minute report. Landlord negotiates: *"I can do that, but it will delay the Compliance Project. Which is the priority?"* (Agency).
8:00 PM	Finally logs off. Exhausted. Numbs out with Netflix. Dreads tomorrow.	Logs off at 5:30. Spends evening with family or working on "The Lifeboat" (Chapter 7). Goes to sleep knowing they have Options.

Table 1 The Autonomous Professional Mindset

FAILURE MODES: THE HUMBLE ENTRY

How to Sabotage Your Own Reinvention

Although you may have the appropriate strategic approach, the psychological strain of the "Zero Point" may result in rational behavior from even the most intelligent and experienced professionals. Observe for these two particular anti-patterns.

1. The "Bitter Genius"

This professional accepts the entry-level job, but declines to accept the entry-level position. They see the job as an affront rather than tuition.

- **The Symptom:** They constantly remind peers of their past. "Well, when I was a VP at [Company], we didn't do it this stupid way." They sigh loudly during administrative tasks.

- **The Result:** The "Corporate Immune System" is activated. Their colleagues view them as toxic and arrogant. They are socially isolated, which hinders their ability to learn the "Hidden Curriculum." They get fired, not due to ineptitude, but for "fitting in culturally."

- **The Cure:** Radical amnesia. You must act as if your past success never happened until you have earned the right to reference it.

2. The "Apologist"

This professional is afraid that others will view them as a failure for taking a job below their level of experience. Therefore, they excessively justify their existence.

- **The Symptom:** Almost every introduction includes a disclaimer. *"I'm doing this temporarily while I search for something better,"* or *"Actually, I was a director."*

- **The Result:** They signal that they are flight-risk. The manager will stop investing in them, assuming the Apologist is planning to leave.

- **The Cure:** Own the narrative. *"I selected this job so I could develop the basic principles of this sector."* Confidence drowns out the room; apologies create noise.

End-of-Chapter Reflection Prompt

Humility: In what specific ways has your work changed *how* you are used by others in the last year?

CHAPTER SIX

FROM SKILL BUILDING TO LEVERAGE

The Mathematics of Competence and the Strategic Generalist

The Concept: The Specialist's Dilemma

For the last century, the dominant career advice has been governed by the shadow of the assembly line: Specialize. We are told to find a niche, drill down, and become the absolute best in that narrow field. In a static economy, this works. In a dynamic economy, It's a trap.

Economically, singular specialization suffers from the **Law of Diminishing Returns**. Imagine learning a new skill-say, Excel.

- **The First 20 Hours:** You learn the interface, basic formulas, and formatting. You are now more competent than 50% of the population.

- **The Next 100 Hours:** You learn pivot tables, VLOOKUP, and basic macros. You are now in the top 10% of users.

- **The Next 10,000 Hours:** To move from the top 10% to the top 1%, you must dedicate years to learning obscure VBA scripting.

The Pareto Efficiency of Learning

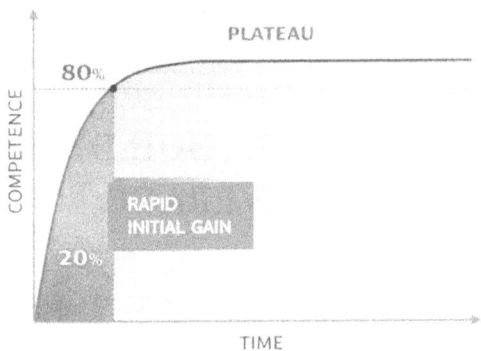

Figure 6.1 The Pareto Efficiency of Learning

This is the **Pareto Efficiency of Learning**. You achieve 80% of the functional value in the first 20% of the time. The strategist stops at 80%, pivots, and starts acquiring a new skill.

The term "Talent Stack" was coined by Scott Adams, who realized he would never be the best artist, nor the funniest writer, nor the smartest businessman. However, he could be in the top 25% of all three.

"Capitalism rewards things that are rare and valuable. You make yourself rare by combining two or more 'pretty good' skills until no one else has your mix."

The Math: Probability and Complementarity

In economics, two goods are "complementary" if possessing one increases the value of the other. The probability of someone being in the top 25% of Group A and Group B is $0.25 \times 0.25 = 0.0625$. By simply being "pretty good" at two things, you are in the top 6% of the hybrid field. Add a third skill, and you are in the top 1%.

The Math: Probability and Complementarity

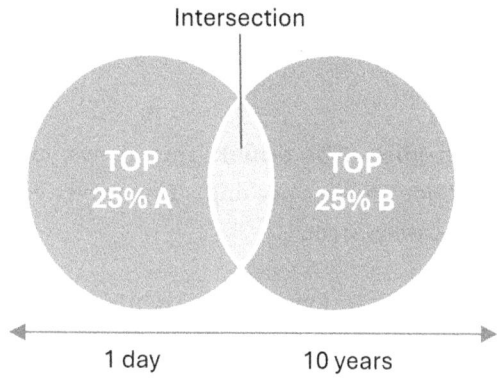

Figure 6.2 *The Probability Advantage*

Wicked vs. Kind Environments

We look to David Epstein's research in Range.

- **Kind Environments:** Rules are fixed (e.g., Chess, Golf). Specialization wins here.

- **Wicked Environments:** Rules change, patterns are messy (e.g., Business, Healthcare). Generalists win here.

The modern career landscape is a **Wicked Environment**. The "Specialist" is fragile; if the rules change, their value collapses. The "Talent Stacker" is antifragile.

The Architecture of a Robust Stack

A true executive stack consists of three distinct layers:

1. **The Foundation (The Domain):** This is your primary trade (e.g., Nursing, Accounting). Without this, you have no legitimacy.

2. **The Bridge (The Function):** This organizes the work (e.g., Project Management, Logistics). This moves you from "Laborer" to "Manager."

3. **The Multiplier (The Scale):** This allows you to broadcast value (e.g., Code, Public Speaking). This moves you from "Manager" to "Executive/Asset."

The Three-Layer Stack Architecture

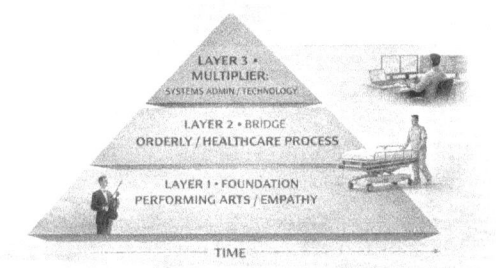

"How three disconnected domains combined to create a unique monopoly."

Figure 6.3 *The Three-Layer Stack Architecture*

THE STACK ARCHITECT

How to Design Skill Architectures That Make You Rare

Most people collect skills like they collect souvenirs-randomly. An Autonomous Professional designs a Stack-a cohesive system where each layer multiplies the value of the others.

The Three-Layer Stack Doctrine

Your stack must follow a strict architectural logic. You need a Foundation, a Bridge, and a Multiplier.

The Canonical Strategic Stacks

Here are three examples of high-leverage architectures:

The Author's Talent Stack

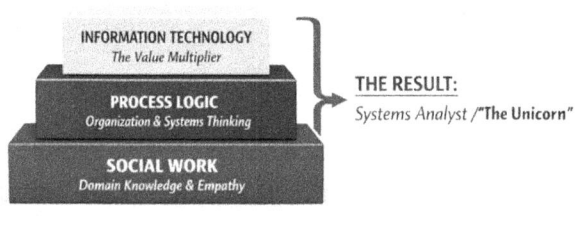

By combining a common domain (Social Work) with a hard skill (IT), a unique market niche is created.

Figure 6.4 The Author's Talent Stack

The **"Bureaucratic Assassin" Stack** (Domain + Compliance + Automation): You know the regulations better than the lawyers (Compliance), and you build scripts to adhere to them automatically (Automation). You become the only person who can navigate the red tape at speed.

The **"Truth Teller" Stack** (Domain + Data + Communication): You understand the core business (Domain), you can pull the raw SQL queries to see what's really happening (Data), and you can present it to the board in clear narratives (Communication). You replace entire analytics departments.

The "Iron Gate" Stack (Domain + Procurement + Vendor Control): You know what the company needs (Domain), and you know exactly how vendors try to overcharge for it (Procurement). You become the gatekeeper of profit.

Stack ROI Testing

Before investing 500 hours in a new skill, run the Replacement Test: If I add this skill, does it make me harder to replace, or just better at my current job?

If it only makes you faster, it's a trap. If it makes you unique, it's a stack.

COMMON FAILURE MODES: THE TALENT STACK

Why Smart People Build Weak Architectures

Building a Talent Stack is not just about "learning more." It's about learning the *right* combination.

1. The "Hoarder" (The Certification Trap)

This professional confuses "Credentials" with "Leverage." They collect degrees and certificates that are all in the same domain.

> **The Symptom:** A resume that lists a BA, an MA, a PhD, and 5 certifications, all in "History" or "Management."

> **The Analysis:** This is not a stack; it's a pile. Adding a 5th certification to a domain you already know is a waste of capital. It yields diminishing returns.

The Cure: You must seek **Orthogonal Skills**. If you are a Writer, don't get a Master of Fine Arts; learn Data Analytics. The value comes from the intersection, not the depth.

2. The "Purist"

This professional refuses to learn the "Bridge" or "Multiplier" layers because they feel it's beneath their craft.

> **The Symptom:** The brilliant coder who refuses to learn "Sales" because "sales is slimy." The great artist who refuses to learn "Marketing."
>
> **The Result:** They remain an Operator forever. They are dependent on others to value their work.
>
> **The Cure:** Accept that "Selling" is not a dirty word; it's the delivery mechanism for your value. Without it, your stack has no output.

End-of-Chapter Reflection Prompt

Leverage: What rationalizations are you using to stay in a role where your growth has quietly stopped?

PART III - THE AUTONOMOUS CAREER

CHAPTER SEVEN

WHEN TECHNOLOGY CHANGES THE RULES

The Economics of Leverage and the Rise of the Intrapreneur

The Concept: The Operator vs. The Analyst

In every organization, the workforce is divided into two economic classes:

- **The Operator (Linear Value):** They execute the core function. Their value is Linear (time for money). Earning potential is capped by the hours in a day.

- **The Analyst (Exponential Value):** They design the workflow. If an Analyst writes a script that automates a task for 100 employees, they generate 50 hours of value with a one-time investment. Their value is Exponential.

The Operator vs. The Analyst

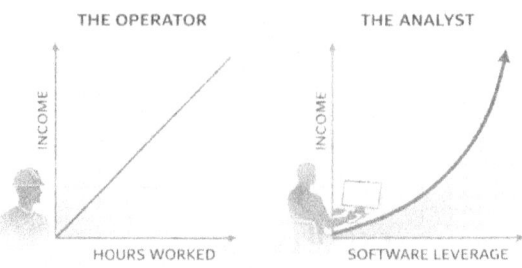

Figure 7.1 Linear vs. Exponential Value

The Career Imperative: To survive, you must migrate from the "Production Layer" (doing the work) to the "Abstraction Layer" (designing the system).

Defining Intrapreneurship

Coined by Gifford Pinchot III, Intrapreneurship is the act of behaving like an entrepreneur within a large organization. The Intrapreneur operates under an "Agency Mindset" rather than a "Permission Mindset." They assume political risk but enjoy subsidized R&D.

The Phenomenon of "Shadow IT"

When the author (a Social Worker) built a database to manage his caseload, he was engaging in Shadow IT. He was solving a "Local Knowledge Problem." The Central IT Department knows technology but not social work. The Social Worker knows social work but not technology. The Hybrid bridges the gap.

The "Hidden Factory"

In every company, there is the "Official Factory" (documented processes) and the "Hidden Factory" (undocumented workarounds). The Hidden Factory consumes 15-40% of a company's capacity. The Operator lives inside it; the Intrapreneur exposes and automates it.

The Hidden Factory Iceberg

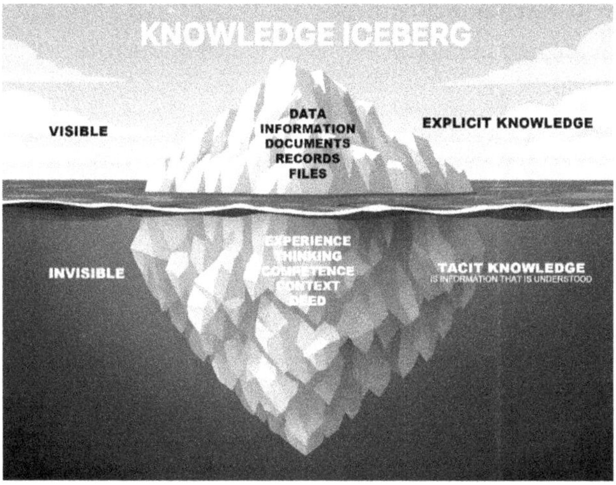

Figure 7.2 The Hidden Factory Iceberg

THE INTRAPRENEUR FIELD GUIDE

How to Build Invisible Monopolies Inside Organizations

Every corporation is actually two companies. The **Official Factory** is owned by the CEO. The **Hidden Factory** is up for grabs.

The Intrapreneur does not ask for permission to innovate. They simply observe the Hidden Factory, identify the chaos, and quietly build the solution. They annex the workflow before anyone realizes it was broken.

The Target Zones

To build your monopoly, hunt in these specific zones:

Data Translation Zones: Find the place where two systems don't talk to each other, and where a human is currently copy-pasting data. Build the bridge. Own the data flow.

Error Repair Loops: Find the department that spends 30% of its time fixing the mistakes of the previous department. Automate the validation.

Compliance Workarounds: Find the spreadsheets that everyone uses because the official software is too slow. Formalize them. Control them.

The Strategy: The "Trojan Horse" Fix

You don't propose a "Digital Transformation Initiative." That requires budgets. Instead, you just "fix the spreadsheet." You write a small script. Then you expand it. By the time IT notices, the entire division is dependent on your code. You have captured the means of production.

THE INTRAPRENEUR'S SCRIPTS

How to Innovate Without Getting Fired

The Intrapreneur walks a dangerous line. If you innovate too quietly, you get no credit. If you innovate too loudly, you trigger the "Corporate Immune System"-middle managers who view change as an indictment of their current competence.

To build your "Invisible Monopoly" (Chapter 5.1), you need to master **Political Jargon**. You must frame your innovation not as "Change," but as "Compliance" or "Help."

Here are the three essential scripts for the Intrapreneur.

Script 1: Gaining Access (The "Help Me Help You" Frame)

Scenario: You need access to a database or a dataset that is currently siloed by IT or another department. If you ask for "data access," they will say no due to security.

- **The Wrong Pitch:** "I need access to the SQL server so I can build a better dashboard than the one we have." (Result: Blocked. You insulted their dashboard).

- **The Strategic Script:** *"I noticed your team gets hit with the same three report requests every Monday. I'd love to take that grunt work off your plate. If you give me read-only access to [Specific Table], I can run those reports locally and just send you the final PDF. It saves you an hour a week."*

- **Why it works:** You offered labor, not threats. You framed access as a way to reduce *their* workload.

Script 2: The "Pilot" Pitch (De-Risking the New Tool)

Scenario: You have built a tool (e.g., an automated scheduling script) and you want to roll it out to the team.

- **The Wrong Pitch:** "I built a system that replaces our manual process. Everyone should switch to this." (Result: Panic. Managers fear downtime).

- **The Strategic Script:** *"I've been running a small 'Sandbox Pilot' on my own desk to handle the overflow. It's successfully processed 500 records without error. I'd like to run it on just 10% of the team's volume next week as a stress test. No change to the main workflow yet-just a side experiment to see if we can catch errors faster."*

- **Why it works:** You used the word **"Pilot."** In corporate speak, a Pilot is safe. It implies reversibility. Managers love Pilots; they hate "Switchovers."

Script 3: The Defense (When You Are Told to "Stay in Your Lane")

Scenario: A manager catches you coding or building systems instead of doing your "core job."

- **The Wrong Defense:** "The current way is stupid and this is faster." (Result: Insubordination).

- **The Strategic Script:** *"I'm strictly focused on hitting my KPIs. I built this tool solely to ensure I never miss a deadline and to ensure 100% compliance with the new audit standards. It's just a personal checklist I use to guarantee quality."*

- **Why it works:** You invoked **"KPIs"** and **"Compliance."** You framed the innovation as a personal dedication to *their* metrics. It's very hard to punish an employee for trying to be "100% compliant."

COMMON FAILURE MODES: THE INTRAPRENEUR

How to Innovate Yourself Out of a Job

Intrapreneurship is high-risk. You are changing the status quo, which threatens people.

1. The "Silent Martyr"

This professional fixes the broken process but tells no one. They automate their own job to save time, then use that time to watch Netflix or do more grunt work.

- **The Symptom:** The department runs smoothly only when they are there. When they take a vacation, everything breaks.

- **The Result:** They have zero leverage. The company assumes the *process* works, not knowing the *person* is holding it together with duct tape. If they leave, the company crashes, but the company doesn't know that yet.

- **The Cure:** You must "Market the Fix." You must present your solution to management. *"I built this tool to save 10 hours. Here is the documentation."* Convert the labor into a visible asset.

2. The "Arsonist"

This professional tries to fix everything at once. They criticize the legacy systems openly.

- **The Symptom:** They send emails titled "Why our current system is broken." They propose a "Total Digital Transformation" in their first month.

- **The Result:** They trigger the "Black Box" defense mechanism. The "Old Guard" (who built the legacy system) destroys them politically to protect their own status.

- **The Cure:** Respect the **Chesterton's Fence** principle: Don't remove a fence until you know why it was put there. Fix small, painful things first to build trust.

End-of-Chapter Reflection Prompt

Technology: Is technology allowing you to solve harder problems, or just helping you repeat the past at a higher velocity?

CHAPTER EIGHT

EXPERTISE AND THE PRE-EMPTIVE STRIKE

Signal Detection, Asymmetric Risk, and The Dead Sea Effect

The Concept: The Dead Sea Effect (Adverse Selection)

All organizations have liquid employees (high performers) that can leave the organization the quickest. When a corporation goes into decline (it gets "Chilled"), those same high performers exit the organization first. Who remains in the organization? The salt — or the residue of mediocrity. Therefore, if you remain in the organization, the marketplace assumes that you are the salt, the mediocre employee (Adverse Selection).

Signal Detection Theory: Noise vs. Threat

Most employees have a Conservative Bias-they dismiss bad news as "noise." The strategist adopts a Liberal Bias toward threat detection.

- The cost of a "False Alarm" (updating your resume unnecessarily) is low.

- The cost of a "Miss" (being fired) is catastrophic.

Asymmetric Risk Profiles

- **"Wait and See" Strategy:** Limited Upside (keep job), Infinite Downside (mass layoff).

- **"Pre-emptive Strike" Strategy:** High Upside (better job), Capped Downside (minor stress).

The Corporate Lifecycle

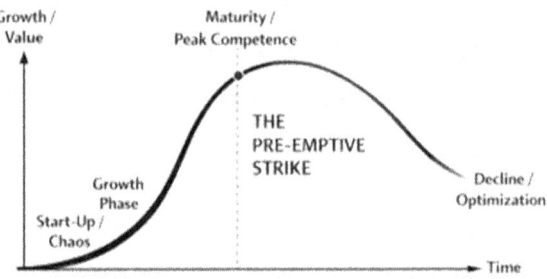

The "Pre-emptive Strike" must occur at the peak of maturity, before the "Optimization" phase erodes value.

Figure 8.1 The Corporate Lifecycle

The Agency Spectrum: Passive Victim vs. Active Agent

- **Passive Victim:** Operates under the "Feudal Model." Believes loyalty buys protection. Waits for the layoff. Enters the market at the point of maximum desperation.

CHAPTER EIGHT | 97

- **Active Agent:** Operates under the "Mercenary Model." Views the company as a client. Constantly audits the company's health. Enters the market when they are strong.

The **"Pre-emptive Strike"** is the act of firing your employer before they can fire you.

The Pre-emptive Strike Payoff Matrix

	STRIKE	NO STRIKE
DISASTER	MITIGATION COST	CATASTROPHE OR HIGH COST
NO DISASTER	GRACE OR LOW COST	ILLUSION OF SAFETY

Figure 8.2 The Pre-emptive Strike Payoff Matrix

THE PRE-EMPTIVE STRIKE RESIGNATION PROTOCOL

How to Leave Without Losing Leverage

The standard resignation is a binary event: Yesterday, you were an employee; today, you are a stranger. This is a waste of leverage.

The Autonomous Professional treats resignation not as a divorce, but as a **Contract Conversion**. Your goal is to convert your status from "Full-Time Employee" (Fixed Cost) to "On-Demand Consultant" (Variable Cost). This helps you populate "The Lifeboat" (Chapter 9) with your first client-your former employer.

The Timing: The "Knowledge Gap" Window

Don't resign when the project is finished. Resign when the project is critical but stable.

- *Too Early:* They panic and burn bridges.

- *Too Late:* They don't need you anymore.

- *Just Right:* The system is running, but *only you* know how to fix it if it breaks. This creates the "Consultant's Curve" leverage.

The Document: The "Bridge" Resignation Letter

Most resignation letters are generic templates. Yours must be a sales proposal.

The Template:

Dear [Boss Name],

Please accept this letter as formal notification that I will be resigning from my position as [Role]. My last day will be [Date].

I am incredibly proud of what we built, specifically [mention the "Black Box" or critical system you own]. I want to ensure that this transition is seamless and creates zero disruption for the team.

To that end, I have prepared a robust handover documentation plan for the next two weeks.

Additionally, knowing that [Critical Project/System] requires specialized historical knowledge, I am open to a limited retainer agreement post-departure to be available for emergency troubleshooting or team training. I have attached a brief proposal for how that might look, should you need that insurance policy.

Sincerely,

[Your Name]

The Psychology of the "Retainer" Proposal

You attach a separate one-page document outlining a "Consulting Retainer."

- **The Offer:** "5 hours of availability per month + 24-hour response time for emergencies."

- **The Price:** 2x your previous hourly rate (or a flat fee).

- **The Sell:** You are selling **Insurance**. The boss is terrified that things will break when you leave. For a small monthly fee, they can buy "peace of mind."

Most bosses will sign this immediately because it solves their immediate panic. You have now successfully executed the **Soft Landing**. You walked out the door, but kept the check.

End-of-Chapter Reflection Prompt

Restraint: What is one "flattering" opportunity you could decline this month to restore your sense of fit?

CHAPTER NINE

THE MYTH OF THE PIVOT IS NO MYTH AT ALL

Modern Portfolio Theory, BATNA, and the Antifragile Career

The Concept: Modern Portfolio Theory for Careers

Economist Harry Markowitz taught us that an investor shouldn't just look at returns, but at correlation. If Asset A crashes, Asset B should rise. Most professionals violate this by practicing Total Concentration (one salary, one employer). A monthly paycheck has low volatility but massive Tail Risk (it can go to zero overnight).

The Antifragile Career

Nassim Taleb defines "Antifragile" as something that gets stronger under stress. A diversified career is antifragile. If you lose your main job, the stress forces you to lean into secondary streams.

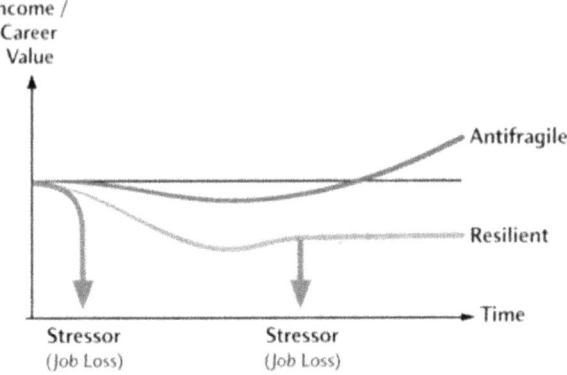

Figure 9.1 The Antifragile Career Curve

Case Study: The Snake Pit and the Lifeboat

The subject managed two asset classes:

1. **The Physical Classroom:** High Political Risk.

2. **The Online Program:** Low Political Risk.

When the "Snake Pit" (political toxicity) destroyed Asset 1, he shifted his portfolio weight to Asset 2. He lost the office, but kept the income.

Strategic Analysis: The Power of BATNA

Your negotiating power is defined by your BATNA (Best Alternative to a Negotiated Agreement).

- **Weak BATNA:** "I can't pay my mortgage if I leave." *Result: Captivity.*

- **Strong BATNA:** "I have other income." *Result: Autonomy.*

AUTONOMOUS INCOME ARCHITECTURE

How to Become Exit-Immune

In the Post-Career Economy, reliance on a single income stream is negligence. You must structure your finances like a resilient IT network.

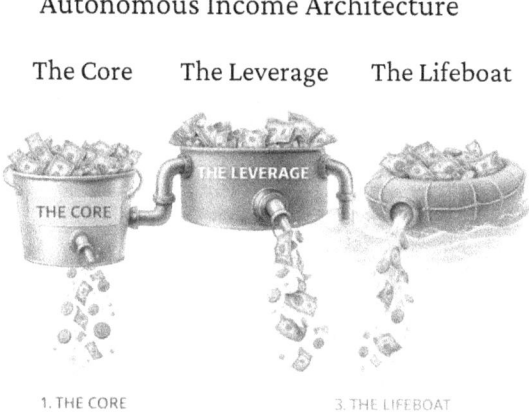

Figure 9.2 *Autonomous Income Architecture*

1. The Core (The Utility)

- **Function:** Primary job. Provides cash flow and benefits.

- **Risk Profile:** High Concentration Risk.

- **Strategy:** Maximize yield, but assume zero loyalty. Use this to fund the other buckets.

2. The Leverage (The Upside)

- **Function:** Scalable income (royalties, dividends, digital products).

- **Risk Profile:** High Volatility, Infinite Upside.

- **Strategy:** This is "breakout" capital. It trades assets for money, not time.

3. The Lifeboat (The Insurance)

- **Function:** Non-Correlated income. Must come from a different industry than the Core.

- **Risk Profile:** Low Yield, High Stability.

- **Strategy:** Keeps the hull floating if the Core collapses. **Correlation Risk is Death. Redundancy is *Autonomy*.**

Once the immediate bleeding has been stopped, the purpose of the lifeboat shifts from survival to stabilization. At this stage, additional income is not about ambition or optimization; it's about buying time, reducing psychological pressure, and restoring optionality. The mistake many professionals make is assuming that income must come from a single, identity-laden source. In both finance and career strategy, security tends to emerge from diversification rather than optimization - small imperfect streams that collectively reduce dependence on any one role or institution.

For some, this takes the form of asset-based income rather than labor. Modest real estate investments - such as renting out a spare room, converting a primary residence into a multi-unit arrangement, or purchasing a small rental property - can transform fixed housing costs into partial income streams. These strategies are rarely glamorous, and they often involve lifestyle compromises, but they have a powerful stabilizing effect: they lower monthly burn while creating income that is not directly tied to professional status. The psychological benefit of knowing that shelter is partially self-funded cannot be overstated.

Others pursue supplemental labor that is deliberately detached from long-term identity. Side work - consulting, tutoring, contract operations, freelance technical tasks, or even non-prestigious service work - functions best when it's treated as infrastructure rather than a future career. The goal is not to build a brand or discover a calling, but to establish predictable cash flow with minimal cognitive load. When supplemental work is framed correctly, it restores agency without draining the energy needed for deeper reinvention.

Equally important are strategies that reduce exposure rather than increase income. Sharing housing, downsizing aggressively, relocating to lower-cost regions, or restructuring family expenses are often dismissed as failures of success. In reality, they are acts of strategic retreat that preserve long-term viability. Lowering fixed costs expands runway. Runway creates calm. Calm enables judgment. These lifestyle decisions are not admissions of defeat; they are balance-sheet decisions made in service of future leverage.

Taken together, these approaches redefine security. Security is no longer derived from a single job, title, or paycheck, but from a web of smaller supports that prevent any one failure from becoming catastrophic. The lifeboat is not meant to carry you forward indefinitely. It exists to keep you afloat while you regain clarity, rebuild strength, and prepare for the next crossing. What comes after stabilization - how to move from survival to deliberate reinvention - is where the work becomes strategic again, and where the narrative resumes its forward motion.

AUTONOMOUS NETWORKING

How to Build a Coalition When You Have No Title

When you have a high-status job, networking is easy. You are a resource. People want to know you because you hold a budget, or influence, or access. You are "The Director." The title does the networking for you.

But when you are in **The Zero Point** (Chapter 1) - when you have left the old career but not yet secured the new one - networking feels like begging.

You dread the standard advice: *"Just ask people for coffee!"* Why? Because the power dynamic is broken. You are the "Asker." They are the "Giver." You are consuming their time (a depleting asset) to ask for a job (a scarce asset). This asymmetry creates the scent of desperation. And in the labor market, desperation is a repellent.

The Autonomous Professional does not "network." They don't "pick brains." They don't ask for favors.

They **Audit Problems**.

The Shift: From "Applicant" to "Consultant"

To fix the power dynamic, you must stop behaving like an unemployed person looking for a savior and start behaving like a Consultant looking for a client.

- **The Applicant asks:** "Do you know of any open roles?" (Low Value / Passive).

- **The Consultant asks:** "I'm researching the friction points in [Industry X]. What is the one problem your team has been trying to solve for six months but can't?" (High Value / Active).

When you ask a person about their problems, two things happen:

1. **You validate their struggle.** (Everyone wants to vent).

2. **You gather "Intel."** You are mapping the **Hidden Factory** (Chapter 6).

You are not asking for a job. You are asking for data. This restores your dignity. You are a researcher, not a beggar.

The Strategy: The Permissionless Audit

The most effective way to network is to do the work before you are hired. Don't wait for an interview to prove your value. Prove it in the cold email. Instead of sending a resume, send an Audit.

The "Audit" Protocol:

1. **Identify a Target:** A person you want to meet in your new industry.

2. **Find a Public Problem:** Read their company's quarterly report, their blog posts, or their LinkedIn rants. Find something broken (e.g., "We are struggling to implement the new compliance standards").

3. **Do the Work:** Spend 4 hours building a solution. Draft a one-page checklist. Write a script. Build a mock-up.

4. **Send the "Gift":** Send it to them with zero expectations.

The Script (The Cold Outreach):

Subject: I made a checklist for your Compliance rollout

> Dear [Name],
>
> I've been following your transition to the new compliance standards. I know from my own experience in [Previous Industry] that this stage is usually a nightmare of documentation.
>
> I took the liberty of converting the new 50-page regulation PDF into a 1-page "Red Flag" checklist. It's what I used to use to keep my teams safe. I attached it here-no strings attached, just thought it might save you some headaches next week.
>
> Best,
>
> [Your Name]

The Analysis:

- You did not ask for a job.

- You did not ask for 15 minutes of coffee.

- You proved **competence** (you understand the regulation).

- You proved **generosity** (you gave an asset).

- **Result:** You have triggered the Law of Reciprocity. They now feel they owe *you* a response. You have flipped the power dynamic.

The Sociology: The Strength of Weak Ties

In 1973, sociologist Mark Granovetter published a study that changed career theory forever: The Strength of Weak Ties. He discovered that most people don't find new jobs through their "Strong Ties" (close friends and family). They find them through "Weak Ties" (acquaintances, friends of friends, former colleagues).

Why? Your Strong Ties possess the same information you do. They live in your bubble. They know about the same job openings you know about. Your Weak Ties live in different worlds. They have access to non-redundant information. They know about the "Hidden Market."

The Network Strategy: Don't waste time commiserating with your close circle. You must aggressively expand your Weak Ties. Reach out to the person you worked with five years ago. Reach out to the vendor you met at a conference once.

The Script (The Dormant Tie Revival):

Subject: Update

> Hi [Name],
>
> I was reading about [News in their industry] and thought of you. I hope you're surviving the chaos.
>
> I'm currently pivoting my focus toward [New Industry] and auditing the landscape. I remember you always had a sharp view on the [Specific Topic] side of things. If you ever have a spare 10 minutes, I'd love to hear your take on where the market is moving.
>
> Best,
> [Your Name]

The Protocol: The Double Opt-In

As you build your network, you will eventually become a "Connector" - someone who introduces two other people.

Warning: There is one rule you must never break. It's the Double Opt-In.

Never introduce two people via email without asking *both* of them first.

- **Bad:** "Hey Jane, meet Bob. Bob wants to pick your brain." (You have just burdened Jane).

- **Autonomy:** Email Jane: *"Bob (a data scientist) asked to meet you. He has some interesting views on [Topic] that align with your current project. Are you open to an intro, or are you heads-down right now? No pressure."*

This protects your social capital. It signals that you respect Jane's time. When you respect high-status people's time, they trust you.

The "Portfolio of Favors"

Networking is not about immediate transactions. It's about banking "Goodwill Equity." Every time you send a helpful article, introduce two valuable people, or solve a small problem for free, you are making a deposit into the Portfolio of Favors.

When you are in the Silent Years, your bank account may be dwindling, but your Portfolio of Favors should be growing. One day, you will need to make a withdrawal (a referral, a reference, a contract). If you have spent six months strictly making deposits, that check will clear.

Stop trying to be "interesting." Start being "useful." Useful people are never unemployed for long.

COMMON FAILURE MODES: STRATEGIC NETWORKING

Why Your Calls Are Going to Voicemail

1. The "Trauma Dumper"

This professional uses networking calls as therapy sessions. They are hurt by their recent layoff and need to vent.

- **The Symptom:** The coffee chat starts with 20 minutes of complaining about their old boss or the "unfair" job market.

- **The Result:** The listener feels drained. They mentally blacklist the professional because they don't want to refer a "negative person" to their own network.

- **The Cure:** Process your grief with a therapist (or your partner), not your network. The networking call must be 100% future-focused and positive.

2. The "Askhole"

This professional asks for advice, agrees with it, but never takes action. Then they ask for more advice.

- **The Symptom:** They email you: *"Can we grab coffee? I'd love your thoughts on X."* You give them a strategy. Two weeks later, they email: *"Can we grab coffee? I'm still stuck."*

- **The Result:** High-value people stop responding. They realize their advice is being wasted.

- **The Cure:** The **"Loop-Close."** If someone gives you advice, don't email them again until you have executed it. *"Hey, I took your advice, did X, and here was the result. Thanks."* This makes the mentor feel powerful and eager to help again.

End-of-Chapter Reflection Prompt

> **(Soft Landing):** If you removed the need for "advancement," what specific contribution would you feel most compelled to offer?

When you are done, you might want to take a step back and consider a trend that is easier to recognize within a group (organization), then in a single entity (person). Organizations, such as businesses, have no sentimental attachment to their identity. If changes occur to the organization's surroundings, the organization will either evolve their structure to match the changes or cease to exist. History is full of businesses that ceased to exist as a result of their refusal to give up their past identity in order to adapt to the changing times by attempting to "work smarter" at that identity, but lost the ability to compete.

A good example of a company that changed its focus from primarily being a hardware manufacturer is IBM. Due to the decrease in profit margins resulting from the increasing commoditization of hardware, IBM chose to disassemble its identity as a hardware manufacturer and began to provide services and consulting and provide large enterprise level software. IBM was able to transform itself from a hardware manufacturing company into a services and software company so effectively because services, consulting and software require a greater degree of judgment, integration and trust than producing and selling physical products.

There are quieter examples, but equally as instructive. For example, Adobe gave up the model of one-time software sales in exchange for a subscription model, in doing so, knowing that they would initially alienate some of their customers in the short term in order to create stable revenue and in line with changing consumption habits. Microsoft, once heavily focused on desktop operating systems, repositioned themselves to focus on cloud infrastructure and enterprise services based on the threat of competition in a rapidly changing environment. These organizations survived and thrived not because of their vision, but because they treated their existing strengths as disposable assets, as opposed to sacred identities.

These organizations share a common thread: restraint, as opposed to innovation. Both companies realized that the products, skills, and structures that made them successful in the past were becoming liabilities in the current environment. They took action before collapse forced the decision. Both organizations used transitional architectures, temporary losses, hybrid models, and internal contradictions to purchase time in order to allow a new core to develop. Neither of these companies asked, "How can we continue to protect who we are?" Instead, they asked, "What must we become in order to be survivable for the next decade?"

While the comparisons to corporations can be painful for individuals, there is a fundamental similarity in the economics. Corporations are allowed to pivot without shame. Professionals are expected to explain, justify, and apologize. However, the underlying economic principles are identical. Markets do not reward loyalty to form, they reward relevance to function. Therefore, the lesson is not to emulate the scale of corporate operations, but the logical operation of corporations: identity follows viability, not the reverse.

As mentioned earlier, the primary purpose of this book has been to illustrate that careers deteriorate before the end of their life cycle and that survival relies on identifying structural changes early enough to respond deliberately. The final chapter focuses on turning the diagnosis into the process of being a steward - how to think beyond the next role or transition and how to be connected to your work, identity, and time in a manner that is coherent regardless of the changing nature of the external world.

It should be noted that not all organizations are capable of transitioning to meet the changing environmental requirements. In fact, many organizations are unable to transition as a result of confusing their historical successes with their potential for future success, a confusion that many professionals experience for the same reasons. Kodak recognized the implications of digital photography before many of their competitors, however, Kodak ultimately could not alter their business due to their inability to abandon their identity as a manufacturer of film. Similarly, Blockbuster defended their brick and mortar stores and late fees long after the consumer behavior had irrevocably changed. In both instances, the leadership knew of the changing environment, but they did not have the permission to abandon the structures, incentives and stories that had previously legitimized their position of power. In the same manner, many professionals act similarly when they refuse to relinquish titles, certifications, or positions that are no longer relevant to the marketplace, confounding loyalty and perseverance with strategic planning. While markets seldom punish ignorance, they do punish delay. While collapse seldom occurs solely as a result of disruption, collapse often occurs as a result of a failure to view identity - whether corporate or personal - as anything other than provisional.

Therefore, the inflection point currently confronting the professional is not a requirement to continually reinvent, but a requirement to intentionally determine which portions of their professional identity must be flexible in order to remain viable over time.

Before moving forward, pause long enough to ask a difficult but clarifying question: Which aspects of my professional identity am I protecting because they are still valuable. And which am I protecting simply because they once were?

CHAPTER TEN

FADE OUT STAGE LEFT

The Lindy Effect, Polanyi's Paradox,
and the Monopoly of the Old

The Concept: The Shift from Growth to Rent

In the final stage of a career, your strategy must shift from Growth (acquiring new skills) to Rent Extraction (charging for access to existing assets).

The Lindy Effect and the Black Box

The Lindy Effect states that the life expectancy of a non-perishable thing is proportional to its current age. A 30-year-old legacy system is safer than a 6-month-old AI tool. By mastering the "Black Box" (proprietary legacy systems), you create a Natural Monopoly.

The Lindy Effect Timeline

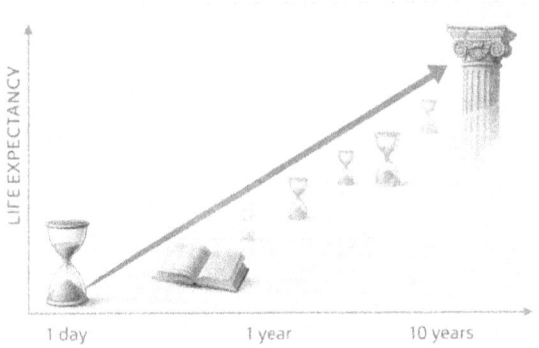

Figure 10.1 *The Lindy Effect Timeline*

Polanyi's Paradox

"We know more than we can tell." Tacit Knowledge (experience) cannot be written in a manual. This is your retention leverage.

EXPANSION: THE CONSULTANT'S CURVE

The Physics of Decoupling Time from Value

As you approach the "Fade Out," you must ascend The Consultant's Curve:

LEVEL 1: THE HANDS (The Technician)

Economic Model: High Effort / Hourly Wage.

Function: You fix the break.

Vulnerability: Linear value. Subject to burnout.

The Consultant's Curve

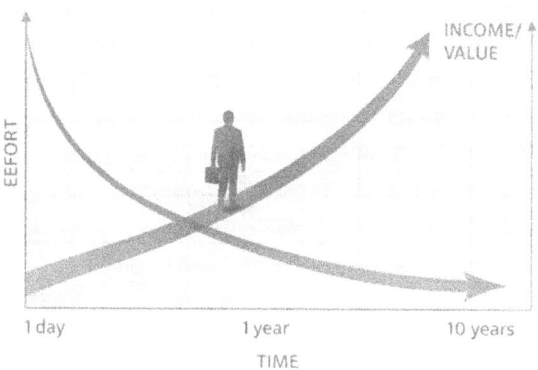

Figure 10.2 The Consultant's Curve

LEVEL 2: THE BRAIN (The Diagnostician)

Economic Model: Medium Effort / High Wage.

Function: You diagnose the break for others to fix.

Strategy: You bill for the diagnosis, not the surgery. You use pattern recognition to solve in minutes what takes others days.

LEVEL 3: THE INSURANCE (The Retainer)

Economic Model: Zero Effort / Pure Profit (Option Value).

Function: You are paid a retainer simply to be available.

The Economics: You are a fire extinguisher. The company pays you because the cost of not having your Tacit Knowledge during a crisis is infinite. You have successfully decoupled time from value.

THE SOFT LANDING DOCTRINE

How Your Final Career Phase Becomes Your Safest

The Soft Landing Doctrine argues for a gradual transition from Laborer (paid for effort) to Insurer (paid for availability). You don't retire; you withdraw labor and keep leverage. You become the "Quiet Authority" who provides the wisdom that prevents disaster.

CONCLUSION

We began this journey at the **Zero Point** - the place where the noise of the world stops and the silence of the "Silent Years" begins. For many, this point is a destination they never chose, a wreckage caused by the collapse of a linear career contract that was never as stable as it seemed.

Throughout this book, we have dissected the mechanics of survival, the architecture of the "Talent Stack," and the economics of the "Pre-emptive Strike." But strategy alone can't save you if the foundation is split.

We must end where we began: with the **Identity Crack**.

The Danger of the Crack

The Identity Crack is that terrifying fissure between *who you were* (The Director, The VP, The Expert) and *who you are today* (The Candidate, The Unknown, The Beginner).

The human mind abhors this gap. It will do anything to bridge it. And its favorite tool for bridging that gap is **Thinking**.

You have likely spent months staring at the crack. You have analyzed your past mistakes. You have hyper-rationalized your future options.

You have treated your career like a math problem that can be solved if you just ruminate hard enough.

You tell yourself this is "planning." It's not. It's **Cognitive Spackle.**

You are trying to fill the void with thought because you are terrified of the reality on the other side. You are using your metabolic energy to sustain a ghost. But here is the hard truth I offer you after forty years of reinvention: **The crack does not close with thinking.**

The "Enough Thinking" Threshold

There is a specific moment in every successful pivot, a moment I call the **"Enough Thinking" Threshold.**

This is the second you realize that *more data will not save you.*

- More introspection will not fix the crack.
- More resume tweaking will not fix the crack.
- More "finding your passion" will not fix the crack.

The crack is only sealed by **New Evidence**. And evidence can only be generated by **Action.**

You can't think your way into a new way of acting; you must act your way into a new way of thinking. The Identity Crack heals the moment you stop "strategizing" about being a consultant and actually sell one hour of consulting. It heals the moment you stop "worrying" about the humble entry and actually scrub into the work.

Action creates the new identity. Thinking merely mourns the old one.

The Sovereignty of the Self

When you finally cross that threshold - when you choose *movement* over *mourning* - you achieve true **Autonomous Professionalism.**

You decouple your survival from the whims of a single institution. You move from being a "Tenant" in someone else's career to being the "Landlord" of your own labor. You become **Antifragile,** a professional who doesn't just survive the shock of a layoff but uses that shock to accelerate into a new, more profitable reality.

The Final Advice

To the professional rebuilding in the dark: **Stop the autopsy.**

You have analyzed the death of your old career enough. Close the file. The repulsion you feel at the "Olfactory Wall," the fear you feel at the "Zero Point" - these are just the symptoms of your old self dying. Let it die.

Earlier, you were asked to consider which parts of your professional identity you were protecting because they remained valuable, and which you were protecting simply because they once were. By this point, the question should feel less threatening and more operational. The goal was never to abandon identity wholesale, but to treat it as a living system rather than a fixed monument. The professional who remains viable over time is not the one who discards their past, but the one who knows precisely which elements can be carried forward, and which must be allowed to expire so that something sturdier can take their place.

If the linear career was a historical anomaly, then autonomy - earned through judgment, adaptability, and restraint - is not a destination, but a practice that must be renewed as long as the world continues to change.

Beneath the title and the status, there is a core of **Internal Dignity** that no layoff can touch and no industry collapse can erode.

The ladder is gone. The horizon is yours.

GLOSSARY OF STRATEGIC TERMS

Antifragile Career: A career structure that gains strength from volatility rather than breaking under it. Unlike a "resilient" career (which merely survives), an antifragile career uses shocks (like layoffs) to accelerate growth via non-correlated income streams.

Autonomous Professional: An individual who has decoupled their economic survival from a single employer. They operate with "Agency," viewing jobs not as identities but as clients.

BATNA (Best Alternative to a Negotiated Agreement): The source of all professional leverage. Your power to negotiate is defined solely by your ability to walk away to a viable alternative (e.g., a second income stream or a pre-existing job offer).

Black Box: A legacy system or process critical to an organization's survival but understood by only one employee. This creates a "Natural Monopoly" for the employee, granting them immense pricing power and job security.

Consultant's Curve: The trajectory of late-career value pricing. It marks the transition from Level 1 (The Hands/Execution) to Level 2 (The Brain/Diagnosis) and finally to Level 3 (The Insurance/Retainer).

Enmeshment: A psychological state where a professional's internal identity is inextricably fused with their external job title. When the job is lost, the self collapses.

Hidden Factory: The undocumented reality of how work actually gets done inside an organization (workarounds, tribal knowledge, error correction). It's distinct from the "Official Factory" (documented processes) and is the primary domain of the Intrapreneur.

Humble Entry Strategy: The strategic decision to voluntarily accept a low-status role to acquire the "Hidden Curriculum" of a new industry. It views the wage cut not as a loss, but as "Paid Tuition" for domain acquisition.

Identity Fracture: The trauma occurring when one's internal self-definition no longer matches their external economic reality. It's often misdiagnosed as depression or burnout.

Intrapreneurship: The act of behaving like an entrepreneur (taking ownership of P&L, innovating processes) while employed within a large organization. This strategy uses the company's resources to subsidize the employee's skill R&D.

Lindy Effect: The theory that the future life expectancy of a non-perishable thing (like a career or technology) is proportional to its current age. A career built on 30-year-old legacy systems is statistically safer than one built on 6-month-old AI tools.

Polanyi's Paradox: The principle that "we know more than we can tell". It explains why deep expertise (Tacit Knowledge) can't be fully documented or automated, serving as the ultimate defense against replacement.

Post-Career Economy: The current economic environment where stability is no longer provided by institutions, and risk has been transferred to individuals. In this economy, the "career" is no longer a structure but a liability.

Pre-emptive Strike: The strategic act of resigning based on market signals (Signal Detection) before a layoff occurs. This preserves leverage and allows the professional to control the narrative of their exit.

Silent Years, The: The psychological and economic "no-man's land" following a career collapse but before a new identity has formed. It's characterized by invisibility and the loss of social gravity.

Talent Stack: The combination of two or more "good" skills (top 25%) to create a unique value proposition that is mathematically rare (top 1%).

Zero Point: The bottom of the reinvention curve where status and visibility are zero, but learning potential is maximum.

RECOMMENDED READING

Part 1 - The Psychology Of Identity

Working Identity by Herminia Ibarra

Why read this: This is the academic bedrock of "Identity Fracture." Ibarra, a professor at London Business School, argues that you can't "think" your way into a new career; you must "act" your way there. She details the "liminal period"-the messy middle between identities-better than anyone else.

Mindset by Carol Dweck

Why read this: Essential for the "Humble Entry." Dweck explains why high-achievers (like the Executive Avatar) struggle to be beginners again. It provides the psychological tools to handle the "Zero Point" without shame.

Big Magic by Elizabeth Gilbert

Why read this: Don't let the title fool you. This is a manual on Perfectionism vs. Production. For the Autonomous Professional building a "Stack," Gilbert's advice on "done is better than good" is critical for avoiding paralysis.

Part 2 - Strategy & Economics

The Portfolio Life by Christina Wallace

Why read this: The definitive modern guide to the "Autonomous Career." Wallace argues that you should not just have a job, but a "portfolio" of identities and income streams. A perfect companion to Volume III.

Thinking in Bets by Annie Duke

Why read this: Duke, a former professional poker player, teaches you how to make high-stakes decisions (like quitting a job) with incomplete information. It reinforces the "Pre-Emptive Strike" methodology.

Pivot by Jenny Blake

Why read this: The tactical field manual for the "Bridge Strategy." Blake breaks down exactly how to run "small pilots" to test a new career direction without blowing up your life.

Part 3 - Foundational Texts

So Good They Can't Ignore You by Cal Newport

The Concept: "Career Capital" (Skills) > Passion.

Antifragile by Nassim Nicholas Taleb

The Concept: Designing systems that gain from disorder.

Range by David Epstein

The Concept: Why generalists triumph in a specialized world.

The Start-up of You **by Reid Hoffman & Ben Casnocha**

The Concept: Treating your career as a beta-stage startup.

Transitions **by William Bridges**

SELECTED BIBLIOGRAPHY

Akerlof, G. A. (1970). "The Market for 'Lemons': Quality Uncertainty and the Market Mechanism." The Quarterly Journal of Economics, 84(3), 488–500.

Arnsten, A. F. T. (2009). "Stress Signalling Pathways that Impair Prefrontal Cortex Structure and Function." Nature Reviews Neuroscience, 10(6), 410-422.

Ashforth, Blake E. Role Transitions in Organizational Life: An Identity-Based Perspective. Mahwah, NJ: Lawrence Erlbaum Associates, 2001.

Autor, David H. "Why Are There Still So Many Jobs? The History and Future of Workplace Automation." Journal of Economic Perspectives 29, no. 3 (2015): 3–30.

Bowen, William G. Higher Education in the Digital Age. Princeton, NJ: Princeton University Press, 2013.

Bremmer, I. (2006). The J-Curve: A New Way to Understand Why Nations Rise and Fall. Simon & Schuster.

Christensen, Clayton M., Michael B. Horn, and Curtis W. Johnson. Disrupting Class: How Disruptive Innovation Will Change the Way the World Learns. New York: McGraw-Hill, 2011.

Conroy, Scott A., and Anne M. O'Leary-Kelly. "Letting Go and Moving On: Work-Related Identity Loss and Recovery." Academy of Management Review 39, no. 1 (2014): 67–87.

Davenport, Thomas H., and Rajeev Ronanki. "Artificial Intelligence for the Real World." Harvard Business Review 96, no. 1 (2018): 108–116.

Dickerson, S. S., & Kemeny, M. E. (2004). "Acute Stressors and Cortisol Responses: A Theoretical Integration and Synthesis of Laboratory Research." Psychological Bulletin, 130(3), 355-391.

Dixit, A. K., & Pindyck, R. S. (1994). Investment Under Uncertainty. Princeton University Press.

Ebaugh, Helen Rose Fuchs. Becoming an Ex: The Process of Role Exit. Chicago: University of Chicago Press, 1988.

Eisenberger, N. I., Lieberman, M. D., & Williams, K. D. (2003). "Does Rejection Hurt? An fMRI Study of Social Exclusion." Science, 302(5643), 290-292.

Eisenberger, Naomi I., and Matthew D. Lieberman. "Why Rejection Hurts: A Common Neural Alarm System for Physical and Social Pain." Trends in Cognitive Sciences 8, no. 7 (2004): 294–300.

Epstein, D. (2019). Range: Why Generalists Triumph in a Specialized World. Riverhead Books.

Feigenbaum, A. V. (1991). Total Quality Control. McGraw-Hill.

Fisher, R., & Ury, W. (1981). Getting to Yes: Negotiating Agreement Without Giving In. Penguin Books.

Frankl, V. E. (1946). Man's Search for Meaning. Beacon Press.

Frey, Carl Benedikt, and Michael A. Osborne. "The Future of Employment: How Susceptible Are Jobs to Computerisation?" Technological Forecasting and Social Change 114 (2017): 254–280.

Gladwell, M. (2008). Outliers: The Story of Success. Little, Brown and Company.

Goffman, E. (1956). The Presentation of Self in Everyday Life. Doubleday.

Granovetter, M. S. (1973). "The Strength of Weak Ties." American Journal of Sociology, 78(6), 1360–1380.

Holiday, R. (2016). Ego Is the Enemy. Portfolio.

Ibarra, Herminia. Working Identity: Unconventional Strategies for Reinventing Your Career. Boston: Harvard Business School Press, 2003.

Kahneman, Daniel, and Amos Tversky. "Prospect Theory: An Analysis of Decision under Risk." Econometrica 47, no. 2 (1979): 263–291.

Koch, R. (1998). The 80/20 Principle: The Secret to Achieving More with Less. Currency.

Koop, R. et al. (2014). "Shadow IT: A Benefit or a Risk?" Proceedings of the 20th Americas Conference on Information Systems.

Kotler, Philip, Hermawan Kartajaya, and Iwan Setiawan. Marketing 5.0: Technology for Humanity. Hoboken, NJ: Wiley, 2021.

Lazear, E. P. (2005). "Entrepreneurship." Journal of Labor Economics, 23(4), 649–680.

Lucas, Henry C., Jr., and Jie Mein Goh. "Disruptive Technology: How Kodak Missed the Digital Photography Revolution." Journal of Strategic Information Systems 18, no. 1 (2009): 46–55.

McEwen, Bruce S. "Physiology and Neurobiology of Stress and Adaptation: Central Role of the Brain." Physiological Reviews 87, no. 3 (2007): 873–904.

Markowitz, H. (1952). "Portfolio Selection." The Journal of Finance, 7(1), 77–91.

Nadella, Satya. Hit Refresh: The Quest to Rediscover Microsoft's Soul and Imagine a Better Future for Everyone. New York: Harper Business, 2017.

Nonaka, I., & Takeuchi, H. (1995). The Knowledge-Creating Company. Oxford University Press.

Pinchot, G. (1985). Intrapreneuring: Why You Don't Have to Leave the Corporation to Become an Entrepreneur. Harper & Row.

Pink, D. H. (2009). Drive: The Surprising Truth About What Motivates Us. Riverhead Books.

Polanyi, M. (1966). The Tacit Dimension. University of Chicago Press.

Ravikant, N., & Jorgenson, E. (2020). The Almanack of Naval Ravikant. Magrathea Publishing.

Rotter, J. B. (1966). "Generalized Expectancies for Internal versus External Control of Reinforcement." Psychological Monographs: General and Applied, 80(1), 1-28.

Sapolsky, R. M. (2004). Why Zebras Don't Get Ulcers. Holt Paperbacks.

Stroebe, M., & Schut, H. (1999). "The Dual Process Model of Coping with Bereavement: Rationale and Description." Death Studies, 23(3), 197-224.

Taleb, Nassim Nicholas. Antifragile: Things That Gain from Disorder. New York: Random House, 2012.

Webster, B. F. (2008). "The Wetware Crisis: The Dead Sea Effect." Bruce Webster on IT.

Zuboff, Shoshana. The Age of Surveillance Capitalism. New York: PublicAffairs, 2019.

Methodology

Healing the Identity Fracture is a nonfiction work for professionals navigating career disruption in a labor market shaped by automation, institutional decay, and identity loss.

The manuscript is grounded in established research across psychology, economics, and organizational theory, but It's written explicitly for a general professional readership. Rather than academic citation density, it prioritizes synthesis, clarity, and practical application. Sources are documented in a Chicago-style Selected Bibliography, and conceptual figures are either original or clearly attributed.

The goal is not to argue theory, but to give readers a usable framework for understanding what is happening to their work - and what to do next - without diluting the intellectual rigor of the analysis.

ABOUT THE AUTHOR

Yale Stern is a retired educator and strategist who spent the forty years comprising his many careers mastering the art of the pivot. His career serves as a masterclass in antifragility, spanning three disparately different industries: the performing arts, healthcare, and enterprise technology.

He navigated his own "Identity Fracture" after a twelve-year career as a professional musician ended, rebuilding his life from the ground up, first as a minimum-wage orderly, then as a licensed social worker, and eventually as a Senior Systems Analyst with an MBA.

He spent the final decade of his corporate tenure as an expert in proprietary legacy systems ("Black Boxes"), proving that the safest place in a modern economy is often the oldest. Now enjoying a "soft landing," he continues to teach and consult on the economics of the self.

APPENDIX A:
THE ARCHITECT'S WORKBOOK

Field Exercises For The Autonomous Professional

Instructions: Don't read this section passively. These exercises are designed to generate the raw data required to re-architect your career. Use a notebook or digital document to answer each module.

MODULE 1: THE IDENTITY AUDIT

(Referencing Chapter 1: Healing the Identity Fracture)

Exercise 1.1: The Identity-Revenue Split Goal: To diagnose the severity of your Role Enmeshment.

1. **Draw a vertical line down the center of a page.**

2. **Column A (The Ego Scorecard):** List the top 5 things that give you a sense of self-worth or identity (e.g., "Leading a team," "Being the expert," "My title").

3. **Column B (The Revenue Scorecard):** List the top 5 activities that actually generate revenue for your company or yourself.

4. **The Audit:** How many items appear in both columns?

Danger Signal: If your "Self-Worth" items (e.g., "Giving speeches") don't match your "Revenue" items (e.g., "Managing spreadsheets"), you are at high risk of Identity Fracture. You are valuing what makes you feel good, not what keeps you safe.

Exercise 1.2: The "Ex-Role" Visualization Complete the following sentences brutally and honestly:

1. "If I were banned from my industry tomorrow, the first asset I would lose is..."

2. "The skill I possess that is most transferable to a completely different industry is..."

3. "My 'Internal Dignity' comes from my ability to [Action], not my title of [Title]."

MODULE 2: THE HUMBLE ENTRY PLANNER

(Referencing Chapter 5: The Humble Entry Field Manual)

Exercise 2.1: The Friction Audit Goal: To identify the best entry point for a new industry.

1. Choose a target industry you wish to enter (e.g., Healthcare, Logistics, Tech).

2. Identify three "Low Status / High Visibility" roles in that industry.

   o *Hint:* Look for roles that handle intake, complaints, or scheduling.

   o **Role Option A:** _____

- Role Option B: _____

- Role Option C: _____

Exercise 2.2: The Hidden Curriculum Checklist Once you enter the "Zero Point" (the entry-level role), your mission is to answer these questions within the first 90 days:

1. Who is the "Shadow Boss" (the person who makes decisions but isn't in charge)?

2. What is the "Third Rail" (the one mistake that gets you fired instantly)?

3. Where is the data manually re-entered (the inefficiency you can automate)?

4. What jargon allows you to pass as a native?

MODULE 3: THE STACK ARCHITECTURE CANVAS

(Referencing Chapter 6: From Skill Building to Leverage)

Exercise 3.1: The Replacement Test List your current top 3 skills. Rate them on "Replacement Difficulty" (1 = Easy to find on Upwork, 10 = Impossible to find).

- **Skill 1:** _____ (Score: __/10)

- **Skill 2:** _____ (Score: __/10)

- **Skill 3:** _____ (Score: __/10)

Exercise 3.2: Build Your Strategic Stack Design a stack that combines three skills to move you into the "Top 1%."

1. **Layer 1 (The Domain):** What is your core trade? (e.g., Accounting)
2. **Layer 2 (The Bridge):** What governs the workflow? (e.g., Compliance/Law)
3. **Layer 3 (The Multiplier):** What scales the output? (e.g., Python/Automation)

   o **The Pitch:** "I am the only [Domain Expert] who can also [Control Skill] and [Scale Skill]."

MODULE 4: THE INTRAPRENEUR'S SCAN

(Referencing Chapter 7: When Technology Changes the Rules)

Exercise 4.1: The "Hidden Factory" Hunt Identify a process in your current job that is broken but "undocumented."

- **The Symptom:** Where do people complain about "double entry" or "waiting for approval"?
- **The Fix:** What simple tool (checklist, script, template) could solve it?
- **The Monopoly:** How can you distribute this tool so that you control the version history?

MODULE 5: THE RISK PROFILE MATRIX

(Referencing Chapter 8: Expertise and the Pre-Emptive Strike)

APPENDIX A: THE ARCHITECT'S WORKBOOK

Exercise 5.1: The Signal Detection Log Review the last 6 months of your company's behavior. Check any that apply:

- [ ] Departure of high-performers (The Dead Sea Effect).
- [ ] Freezing of budgets or travel.
- [ ] Increased demand for reporting/metrics over actual output.
- [ ] Leadership emphasizes "Loyalty" over "Results."

o **Scoring:** If you checked 2 or more, you are in the Danger Zone. Initiate Pre-emptive Strike protocols.

Exercise 5.2: The BATNA Calculation

1. **Current BATNA:** If you walked away today, exactly how many months of runway do you have? _____ months.

2. **Target BATNA:** What "Lifeboat" income source can you start this weekend to extend that runway by 2 months?

MODULE 6: THE AUTONOMOUS INCOME ALLOCATOR

(Referencing Chapter 9: The Myth of the Pivot is No Myth at All)

Exercise 6.1: The Correlation Check List your income streams and their industry source.

1. **Stream 1 (Core):** $_____ (Source: _____)

2. **Stream 2 (Leverage):** $_____ (Source: _____)

3. **Stream 3 (Lifeboat):** $_____ (Source: _____)

   o **Analysis:** If Stream 1 and Stream 2 are in the same industry (e.g., Tech Salary + Tech Consulting), you are NOT diversified. You are concentrated. Identify a Stream 3 that is **Non-Correlated** (e.g., Real Estate, Government Bonds, Manual Service).

MODULE 7: THE CONSULTANT'S CURVE PLANNER

(Referencing Chapter 10: Fade Out Stage Left)

Exercise 7.1: The "Black Box" Inventory Identify the "Legacy Assets" in your organization that only you understand.

1. Is there a piece of code written 10 years ago?

2. Is there a client relationship that relies entirely on your personal history?

3. Is there a regulatory loophole you discovered?

Exercise 7.2: The Retainer Pitch Script Draft the opening line of your "Fade Out" negotiation: *"I am ready to step back from the daily operations (Level 1 work). However, because I am the only one who understands [Black Box Asset], I propose a retainer of $_____/month to remain available for emergencies, ensuring zero downtime for the firm."*

APPENDIX B:
THE CAREER JUDGEMENT CHECKLIST

A framework for evaluating transitions, managing endings, and ensuring experience compounds.

Phase 1: The Diagnostic (Is it time to move?)

Before deciding *where* to go, use these questions to determine the health of your current role:

- **Compounding vs. Resetting:** Does this work increase my future ability to choose, or does it merely reward my endurance?

- **The Identity Test:** Am I describing my role in abstract or managerial terms that feel like I'm talking about someone else's life?

- **The Stagnation Signal:** Is my experience still changing the nature of my work, or is it just proving I can repeat the past well?

- **The Technology Check:** Is the technology I use increasing my capacity to adapt, or just the speed at which I repeat routine tasks?

Phase 2: Evaluating the Risk

Transitions are rarely about finding a "perfect" role; they are about managing the risks of staying versus leaving.

- **The Cost of Staying:** If I stay for another year, will my external network thin and my confidence in my portability fade?

- **Status vs. Worth:** Am I resisting a change because I fear a "status inversion," or because the new role actually lacks intrinsic worth?

- **Economic vs. Social Meaning:** Does this move prioritize economic survival, social meaning, or both? (Note: it's acceptable to choose survival work as a bridge, provided you don't narrate it as a verdict on your worth).

Phase 3: The Filter of Restraint

In mid-to-late career, the challenge is often saying "no" to opportunities that don't fit your integrated identity.

- **The Availability Trap:** Am I considering this role because it fits my values, or simply because it's a role I *could* get?

- **The Energy Audit:** Does this opportunity consume my identity without extending it?

- **The "Obligation" Check:** Am I saying "yes" to reassure others (and myself) that I am still relevant?

Phase 4: Forward-Looking Reflection

As you design your next chapter, ensure it aligns with the goal of "work without a career".

- **Transferability:** If this specific environment disappeared tomorrow, what durable judgment would I take with me?

- **Contribution Mode:** Does this role allow me to apply my judgment to help a system, rather than using the system to advance my personal status?

- **The Final Alignment:** Am I using work as a vehicle for a coherent life, or am I trying to make my life fit the demands of a role?

A Note on Timing: Knowing the difference between compounding and resetting work does not always force an immediate change-but it restores your power of choice.

The Final Advice: To My 30, 45, and 60-Year-Old Selves

- **To the 30-Year-Old:** Don't fear the survival phases. They are the only time you will truly learn that your worth is independent of your title. Build your "Leverage" early.

- **To the 45-Year-Old:** Watch for the Identity Fracture. Don't trade your integrity for a status you will eventually want to walk away from. Learn to say "No" before you have to.

- **To the 60-Year-Old:** You are the Steward now. Your value isn't in how much you can do, but in how much you can see. Describe the horizon for the rest of us.

www.ingramcontent.com/pod-product-compliance
Lightning Source LLC
Chambersburg PA
CBHW060507030426
42337CB00015B/1786